EXQUISITELY BORED

Finding Fulfillment in Retirement

JOANNE L. CLARK

Lucky Book Publishing

"Exquisitely bored is the opposite of the glorification of busyness; it is the process of taking intentional, purpose- ful action to honour and uphold your authentic self."

– Joanne Clark

MY GIFT TO YOU

I am so glad you're here!

As my gift to you, get FREE access to the audiobook of Exquisitely Bored: Finding Fulfillment in Retirement by scanning the QR Code below or visiting

www.exquisitelybored.com/the-book

TABLE OF CONTENTS

PRAISE FOR EXQUISITELY BORED

A radical rethinking of retirement.

Here's a book that caught me off guard, and trust me, you need to read it long before you're thinking about retirement.

Joanne Clark has a fresh take on something most of us dread: that looming question of "What happens when I'm done working?" Instead of the tired old narratives, she introduces us to the "exquisitely bored," brilliant and rebellious people who've decided that decades of hard-won expertise shouldn't just evaporate at 65.

I loved how practical the book is. Clark's "RISE" framework (retire, insight, seek and earn) is inspiring. Instead of retirement being the end of your productive life, it becomes the launching pad for something even better — and profitable too.

I think this book speaks to everyone. Whether you're 35 and retirement feels like a distant worry, 55 and starting to feel overlooked at work, or 65 and realizing that daily golf isn't quite the paradise you imagined -

Clark offers both vision and concrete steps to reimagine this whole phase of life.

This is a rebel's manifesto for anyone who refuses to believe their best contributions are behind them.

– Brad J. Henderson, best–selling author of "The Consistency Effect: How to Turn Reliable Actions into Remarkable Results" and Leadership Coach

What a great read!

I wore a uniform for 27 years and a suit for 23, I am old and I am knowledgeable. I was successful and I know a guy, many I might add. I also know I still have lots to contribute. I just need to figure out how. Joanne worked for me and solved many problems for me and my organization, and this book has just helped me figure out one more: mine!

– Ron Kelusky, Assistant Deputy Minister and Chief Prevention Officer Ontario (ret)

This book is a revolution to retirement!

Joanne's book "Exquisitely Bored" has a unique perspective on retirement. I say: It's about time that retirement is being presented in a totally different way! As an entrepreneur since the age of 21, now close to my 40s, I have never related to retirement. All of the fear-based narratives "warning" me to secure myself for old age always made me feel like people were just waiting to die slowly, it seemed. Joanne nailed so many views and teaches people how to LIVE their lives. I love her self-awareness teachings and bringing the reader to self-care as well. I recommend this to all, even if you are just starting out in your 20s so that you can see how this old way of thinking about retirement can end right now!

– Ellie Laliberté, award-winning international author of "Letters From You to You" & Self–Awareness Coach

A thought-provoking and inspiring perspective on retirement.

By encouraging readers to shift their mindset and actively design this next chapter, it redefines retirement not as an end, but as a vibrant journey of self-discovery, lifelong learning, and meaningful contribution.

– Ben Waldon, CIM, CFP, FCSI Senior Wealth Advisor, Portfolio Manager Scotia Wealth Management

A fresh perspective!

"Exquisitely Bored" offers a fresh perspective on aging, emphasizing purpose, continuous growth, and redefining retirement. It inspires a vibrant, relevant life beyond societal norms, empowering us all to live fully, something that aligns so well with me.

– Shelley A. Murdock, author of "In Search of Longevity", and longevity coach

Smart and soulful!

This book is a mic drop on the myth of retirement! "Exquisitely Bored" is bold, liberating, and exactly what we need to reimagine the "what's next" chapter, not as a wind-down, but a full-on glow-up. It's smart, soulful, and just irreverent enough to shake you out of autopilot. If you've got that "Is this all there is?" itch, this one's speaking directly to you.

– Julee Sung, author of "Thrive and SHINE: A Practical Guidebook for Early–Stage Professionals"

Such an inspiration!

28 years ago, when I was 60, I decided to retire. A colleague warned me, "Don't do it! The actuarial tables say that you will probably be dead in 2 to 3 years."

Had I known Joanne then, I would have invited my "bored" friend to meet her and hear all about exquisitely bored retirement. Now, after we have experienced almost three decades of a fulfilling retirement, my wife and I can wholeheartedly confirm and endorse the vision that inspires this book.

– Robert Polzin, Professor Emeritus and Former Director of the School of Comparative Literary Studies, Carleton University, Ottawa, Canada

A mesmerizing and insightful read.

This book offers a fresh perspective on retirement— reminding us that embracing new beginnings starts with honouring the endings with an open heart.

– Kim Blair, Program Manager Hydro One Networks Inc. (ret.)

A beautiful reimagining of what comes next.

Joanne Clark's book is a powerful and hopeful reframe of retirement... not as an ending, but as a continuation. It invites us to pause and consider that this next chapter isn't about winding down, but about bringing our whole self forward.

By the time we reach retirement, we carry decades of lived experience, hard-earned wisdom, and a deeper understanding of who we are. This book honors all of that. It reminds us that retirement is not a void to be filled with busywork. Instead, it's an opportunity to shape our days with intention. To finally ask: What do

I want this chapter to mean? What do I want to give my time, my energy, and my heart to, now that I have more say in it?

With quiet contemplation and compassionate insight, the author offers a guide to embracing these later years with renewed purpose. There is inspiration here. Not just to do more, but to be more connected to ourselves and what matters most. It's about making meaning, not just managing time.

This book is for anyone wondering what's next. Not in fear, but in freedom. And it's a deeply hopeful companion for those ready to live this next season not by default, but by design.

– Vivian Meraki, author of "Parenting Through Divorce", Human Connection Speaker, Certified Somatic Coach, Founder of Unshakable Parenting

....

This book is both validating and transformative.

Finally, someone has articulated what many of us have felt but couldn't quite name! Joanne's "Exquisitely Bored" is a revolutionary manifesto that dismantles the antiquated notion of retirement as society's finish line. As someone who instinctively rejects age-based limitations and believes we have so much more to offer than outdated social constructs suggest, I found this book both validating and transformative.

At a pivotal moment in human history when we're questioning everything from work-life balance to gender roles, Joanne courageously tackles one of our most deeply embedded assumptions: that our value diminishes with age. Her concept of being "exquisitely bored" isn't about dissatisfaction; it's about recognizing the profound potential that lies dormant when we accept society's script instead of writing our own.

This isn't just a book about retirement; it's a call to arms for anyone who refuses to be defined by arbitrary timelines. Joanne's RISE framework (Retire. Insight. Seek. Earn.) offers a practical roadmap for transforming what society sees as an ending into what it truly is: a magnificent beginning. Essential reading for anyone ready to redefine their next chapter on their own terms.

– Hal S. Eisenberg, L.M.S.W., CEO The Eisenberg Leadership Academy, bestselling author, "Whispers in the Rain: 48 Lessons on the Roadmap to Love and Enlightenment"

DEDICATION

This book is for Henry, the lovely man who sells day-lilies outside of Buckhorn, Ontario. Henry came to Canada in 1955 from the Netherlands. He grew up on a farm and always had a relationship with the land around him. Henry can relate to the restoration and healing that nature provides. Henry retired at 50 due to a health issue, at which time his wife gave him a book on daylilies and he never looked back. Henry started with 6 plants and has now planted over 100,000 daylilies that bloom each summer in waves, for as far as the eye can see. Henry tends to his daylilies from sunrise until sunset, and he can often be seen digging and splitting his creations along the highway as he has now run out of space! His sandwich board at the end of his driveway signals to passers-by that he is open for business: "Day Lilies for Sale." In retirement, Henry has found fulfillment and purpose through sharing his gift of gardening, his talent for creating beauty and his vision for a dream that even a property line cannot quell! At 87, Henry embodies the exquisitely bored spirit with the principles and passion he brings to our community. People either discover him by simply driving by or through word of mouth. He is the most wonderful example of a fulfilled retirement and a life full of meaning! I hope some of you have been blessed enough to have a token of Henry's exquisitely bored in your gardens!

MY INSPIRATION

I never set out to write this book, but as the Exquisitely Bored brand grew, I realized how the concept of my experience would make an interesting fit with how I see the world through home style, décor and beautiful interiors. As I further aligned my passion and principles to write about beautiful spaces, I suddenly saw the natural progression for the book. After all, I was living the brand, and the brand quickly became about how to mobilize to do what you love as your second act and to realize your earning power as you do so. What then if I was able to inspire and incent others to do the same? I was seeing so many talented and skilled people around me in retirement, so it only made sense that it would be a success if I could get my message out and more people could realize their ambitions towards something new. I was also inspired by some of the exquisitely bored examples around me, which were living proof of career continuation on their own terms. Plus, the younger generation would have an account to read about that hopefully would educate and reassure them that it's a fading construct, the whole idea of traditional retirement. Perhaps it would give them more hope, more power and more importantly, permission to entirely rethink retirement in its current form. The book would then become a product under the Exquisitely Bored parent brand and help others realize a new world, beautifully decorated with their talent and skills!

As I continued to write, the book emerged as an obvious way to challenge and inspire everyone, no matter your age or career path, about the notion of retirement in the traditional sense. Whether you are mid-career, nearing retirement or have been retired for a while, I want to encourage conversation and thinking around viewing retirement as your "what's next" in the hope that you can experience fulfillment and meaning in all stages of life. Finding your exquisitely bored in your next term is the pursuit of matching principles and passion and finding your people to experience profound change as you weather the phases of retirement.

For too long we have been limited by traditional constructs regarding retirement, lifestyle and expectations that go along with the old and dated definition of what this life stage should look like. My call to action for RISE, retire, insight, seek and earn, means we can find satisfaction and reward post-career using our skills and talent to continue earning and optimizing our potential. The exquisitely bored are a unique demographic, and my dream is to inspire everyone to realize your exquisitely bored potential even if you are just thinking about retirement and what that can look like. My dream is to shed traditional definitions of retirement so that younger generations have hope, inspiration and ambition to pursue many potential roles for earning power throughout their career into their later years. To dream of a world where we appreciate, support and align with all generations to share learning, experience and input so that we may collectively benefit our communities.

I dream that this book will promote new discussions, new perceptions and new possibilities for all ages. I envision a modern, more accepting reality for how we perceive an older generation and the skills they have mastered. A reality that will enrich job professions, products and services and provide fresh new thinking as well as validation for tried-and-true methods based on experience. I dream of conversations for those who are not fulfilled in their retirement so that we can inspire them to find avenues to work in a capacity that still values and requires their input. But we all need to work to change the narrative, the dialogue and the perceptions together. Effort in the form of a movement can shape new cultural norms and healthier mindsets. I dream of this for you, whoever you may be, that you can find your exquisitely bored and the magic it holds for you!

PROLOGUE

My Exquisitely Bored Story

My story started 20 years ago, when my husband and I made the decision to become part of the movement commonly referred to as FIRE: Financial Independence, Retire Early. From day one of retirement, I went through each and every one of the phases I describe in this book. I was absolutely on the ride of my life without understanding yet that we would be at the forefront of a new movement I've coined as RISE: Retire, Insight, Seek and Earn. You will see alignment with that acronym in the following chapters where I describe the phases.

Through my anecdotal accounts with other retirees, I soon learned that these phases are all too common, unique to each person but exactly what I describe. It would end up being my own anecdotal study within the laboratory of the wild and wide world of retirement lifestyle! One thing I did notice is not many would talk in depth about their retirement struggles. To me, there seems to be a barrier to communication, and I'm wondering if there is a futile feeling for some in the retirement demographic. As I outline in the book, societal constructs are limiting and non-permissive when it comes to deeper exploratory conversations around what retirement can look like. I think this hesitancy is tied to the fear of appearing ungrateful, plus the pressure to be positive and uplifting about this stage of life. Ultimately, I don't think many are able to express or articulate exactly why they have the feelings they do in the phases I describe. Also, if your peers are still working, how can you complain about your state when everyone has the aspiration to be retired? After all, it's what we've been taught based on established and conventional norms tied to age.

The darkest, most painful phase for me was The Shift. Taking action and aligning with my heart was scary, confusing and depressing. I couldn't see the excitement yet and there was no one to share it with. Like I state, it's highly personal, and the only person who can align you is YOU. What I did discover is that once I found the route to start Exquisitely Bored, people were interested and inquisitive. My story was received resoundingly well and the more I shared, the more my own raw, authentic energy would flow and in turn connect me to the people I needed to create my business. That truly manifested for me in the Law of Attraction chapter. I had access to executive coaching throughout my career, I had also experienced our own relationship *Inward Bound* counselling related to heart living, and I was familiar with the concept and its merit. However, nothing prepared me for the depth and breadth of emotional tenacity that this life phase would require of me. I had been curating my personal Exquisitely Bored Instagram handle for a long while, which is a focus on the beautiful, everyday things around us, namely interior design, architecture, lifestyle imagery and décor. I enjoy staging inspiring vignettes from my own homes as an outlet for my insatiable design and décor addiction! It also provided a source of expression for my creative photography and my desire to support and bring awareness to local businesses selling lifestyle products and services. Social media continued to provide a platform to feed my obsession with everything art, interior design, architecture and culture. There is no distance I will not go to for the right decorative detail pertaining to home décor and accessories!

My time spent in other countries at the start of retirement was both inspirational and enlightening as it opened up an avenue for me to see beauty and joy in new environments. From there my heart became so open and receptive that I was able to develop a clear line of sight to where I could lend my skills and talent in retirement. Exquisitely Bored would become a business based on writing and creating content for the interior design and lifestyle sectors. I would provide *words for beautiful spaces.* When I write about how things can evolve throughout the various phases of retirement, that also is from first-hand experience. Clients noticed and began to trust in my deeper, broader background as it relates to all things marketing, public relations and technology. Client after client started appreciating and supporting my skill set and saw what it could bring to their brands as well. Moving from a dark place of The Shift into the light of creative expression, working on my own terms and finding deep fulfillment in my everyday work for Exquisitely Bored as a brand, is truly everything I have manifested.

One of my early mentors had planted the seed of the book, along with the notion of speaking engagements, as being an ideal fit for the Exquisitely Bored brand. Over time, I became strongly persuaded about the retirement process and how I see the world responding to it. It brought peace, vision and passion to put words to what I believe will be the RISE movement. Younger generations are struggling, traditional retirement is not realistic, and current retirees find themselves challenged socially and emotionally, not just financially. It is a movement across multiple generations, and the more we cross-pollinate in and among our various age groups, we can bring great change, hope and prosperity based on a new revolution for how we see retirement.

Exquisitely Bored is a mindset; it's also a demographic of people. It's about seeing the world in its everyday beauty, and appreciating being bored doing wonderful things. But it's not the traditional definition of bored. It's about finding the things that match your principles and passion and including the people you need around you to make it happen, so it doesn't feel like work. Find value in what you do. It's okay to make money doing what you love and in your new life term! Your skills and value should absolutely be traded for financial gain and your empowerment will be the reward. If I can impart one thing to you as the reader, start changing the narrative, start using new positive dialogue around retirement, start seeing the potential for what your exquisitely bored can be no matter your age. You are not an age, you are not a pension number, you are more than random drinks and charcuterie boards on Tuesdays. You are not just a pickleball player, you are more than a card game at the Legion. You are an achieving, creative, brilliant mind with ideas and courage. I hear you, I celebrate you, I see you RISE!

CHAPTER 1
WHO ARE THE
EXQUISITELY BORED?

"Do not go willingly into the ordinary;
awaken, accept and shift."
– Exquisitely Bored

Who are the exquisitely bored? They are not an age, they are not one style, they are not one size and they certainly are not predictable. The exquisitely bored are amongst us. The exquisitely bored are retired, about to retire or have a longer path to their freedom intersection. The exquisitely bored are interested in one thing: *What's next for me?* They possess an incredible amount of talent and a surplus of drive and initiative. They know there is more of the good stuff in life and are willing to take action. They know their scope of talent and are arguably some of the most self-aware people you will ever meet. The over-thinking and the struggle to find that next thing is all-consuming, and for those of you still thought-provoked by heart and intuition, who don't even know you are exquisitely bored, prepare yourself for one of the most beautiful transitions you will ever experience in your life. The magnitude of the transformation is complicated and complex at times. However, finding a place for your skills and finally recognizing your talents and turning that to action to share with the world is not only rewarding but deeply fulfilling and profound. Finding this fulfillment and meaning in your retirement phase is about contributing, continuous learning and staying relevant. It's about finding satisfaction and staying connected in your post-career life while living to your full potential.

Not a Clear Path

When retirement in the traditional sense presents itself either at the right time or as something forced, it's often not a straight road and can be fraught with conflicted emotions. Retirement was always something on that really bad work day that you just couldn't wait to experience. It also takes an enormous amount of planning and preparation. When time and energy go into such an important life phase, it can be disappointing to realize it's not exactly what one expected.

The traditional notion of retirement is gradually shedding its stereotype, but most just keep working in the same context but perhaps lighten the load. This option definitely fits the bill for continuous learning and mindful stimulation. There is still a group for which the work role no longer fits. You've purchased your seasonal home and the desire for continual business travel and a scheduled work week is no longer appealing. Your financial situation has offered you the flexibility of freedom, and work in the traditional sense is now driven by other factors and not money. It's time to hang up our notion of antiquated retirement to see the world through the lens of *what's next.* Instead, the process becomes an evolution of ourselves, emotionally and psychologically. We may even share time with the traditional work world along with other pastimes, spending time and energy in both. Today's reality has us living longer, managing health in new and innovative ways, and ultimately keeping us in the game of life longer.

Defying Expectations

Retirement has typically been associated with an age. Here in Canada, it's 65 with the option of taking your Canada Pension Plan earlier at 60. And for some of you reading, does that not manifest as living life on a continuous calendar of counting down to your 60s? And what about those who are able to retire at an even earlier age? Society has done a really good job of supplying a hamster wheel of goals driven by mere age. The Retirement Countdown App tracks your retirement countdown on your home screen using customized background photos. The widget of daily notifications reminds you of how long until your big day. Beautiful background images build an expectation and perception of what this big, fabulous day will be like! But what if we were to start thinking of our life in terms of one continuous span? We could have goals driven by continuous learning spread out in stages throughout our entire career life. What if we were to challenge the age barrier and instead refer to retirement as an entry or a term? An entry into our *what's next.*

We spend a lifetime and a career focused on gaining education, developing skills and piling on real world experience. The talent and abilities that people have amassed is mind blowing. If you were to think of this accumulated experience packaged up into an education offering, it would cost you unparalleled amounts of money! How taken for granted does this all become when we are simply living for an age goal? Any idea what that fixed thinking does to our brain? The limited thinking, the dark and almost crippling thought that at a certain age, one would be just simply done.

It doesn't help that ageism has played a large part in discounting and deleting workers and their skills. This being put out to pasture is something that women in particular have had to field. We've managed our insecurities with Botox, filler and laser treatments and have gone to pasture in physically beautiful ways.

Let's take the same initiative and investment and apply it to nurturing our work souls in ways that are conducive to finding our *what's next.* What if we were to start thinking about the *what's next* while we are still working? Think of the directional skill set we could build throughout our traditional work life that would prepare us for the entry point of *what's next.* But it's okay not to know what our *what's next* is. It's not about putting pressure on ourselves to know. Some will know right away and some will not. This read is about the discovery process, and if it helps those at a younger age think in terms of a later entry point, then mission accomplished. Can you imagine a world where we build our ideas of *what's next* into our actual retirement planning? That it would become second nature and part of the process, to prepare for our next term once financial freedom was found. We must not be so sheep-like from the get go. We can't change systemic structure overnight, but we can find and inspire the exquisitely bored to take action, find more meaning and experience greater fulfillment.

The exquisitely bored are a powerful demographic that will change and shape the future of society. The buying power, as well as the product and service offering of this target market, can empower and enrich our communities and future generations. The exquisitely bored are proud and passionate about their past. They have spent years honing skills, re-inventing themselves in careers, practicing entrepreneurship in some cases; they have bought and sold companies, they have worked for bosses, managed all generations and have resumes that read like novels. The power of reaching your freedom intersection is a game changer. If you understand the journey and the phases, you can tap into your ambition, future desire and aspirations in ways never thought possible. This book is an account of the phases one may encounter as they approach or are presented with the notion of traditional retirement. Throughout each phase, it suggests new methods and ways of thinking to challenge the traditional linear way in which we are accustomed to perceiving retirement.

Not Birds Of A Feather

What makes the exquisitely bored even more unique is that, because of today's remote work world, they could be anywhere. If you can tap into what you are really good at, and I mean really use your talents, you can work from anywhere, share your product or service offering and absolutely love what you are doing. If you relax into it, believe it, try it on for size, then you will most definitely see the money follow. Write it, build it, paint it, fix it, invent it, but first from your heart. It's not about survival; it's about enjoying and living in your state of utter fulfillment because of what you further lend your skills and your talents to in your next term. The exquisitely bored are not the same age. They don't dress the same, they don't eat the same things and they don't consume the same content. They will be one of the most elusive and unique groups within society and our communities. They are chasing a feeling and things that are so vastly different for each individual, that all they can really relate to at the end of the day is that they all had a journey. Their journeys all likely unfolded with the exact same realization though, that retirement is not just about finances; it's about finding new ways to achieve fulfillment and satisfaction using your skills, talent and aspirations to find new meaning.

It's Not An Age

Society has always based the definition of retirement around age. You get old, you retire. There are books on re-inventing yourself in retirement, self-help books on finding your "why," specific counselling for retirees, and the list goes on. But it always falls to some particular service or product that people of a certain age are thought to engage with. We have an enormous amount of wealth being made in tech booms, product innovation, real estate, emerging products and services, acquisitions and currencies on the block chain, all sorts of methods to the madness. With that come younger generations with wealth who gain financial freedom outside of the predicted age norm. The exquisitely bored can be anyone reaching that point of utter and complete confusion about their *what's next.*

As a Generation X, I look around me and I do see examples of this emerging demographic. However, for the most part, everyone before and up to my generation seem to fall into the conventional mold of retirement. Even when we buy into what a retiree is supposed to look like, it's all so dismal. The clothes, the hair, golf playing beer bellies, bingo at the Legion, curling in winter and the Florida retiree with the tropical shirt and the pacemaker. I think we are still somewhat caught in this trap of solitary confinement of the mind for retirement psychographics. From what I see out there, not a lot has changed on the surface. But I know what lies beneath is percolating, and the birth of a new narrative and disruptive thinking is taking place. I think there are increasingly more of us, but the self-confidence and the leap of faith it takes to embrace your *what's next* can be paralyzing. The migration from the big city to more rural areas is creating opportunity and exposing people to more creative thinking, which is also contributing to the exquisitely bored finding their way to new ideas and potential. We likely need to drop the term entirely, which is the play on words that exquisitely bored connotes.

One can understand the opposite of the glorification of busyness and see that being exquisitely bored is a very mindful state. A state of enjoying exquisitely wonderful things that are of interest to you personally. Exquisitely bored is the state of wondering what's next, in terms of work, life pastimes and potential contribution. The contribution to yourself, your feelings of fulfillment and how to share your talents. There are many resources regarding discovering and sharing our gifts. But this goes beyond that. The concept of the exquisitely bored is more about the process and inner fulfillment that comes when we become humble and open to discovering bigger things and thinking, in a later stage of life. And what if this was combined with financial reward, that you could realize a value exchange for using your various skills and talents in new and useful ways?

The exquisitely bored are not limited by age. They still may be limited by a bank account and can't build a company overnight, but the skill set attached to such initiatives is not small in most cases, so finding the people and connections to make your big thinking happen is all part of the process. What happens when the exquisitely bored find one another? The ties and relationships that are born are only a network away from any and all possibilities. The idea that you are supposed to do this all on your own is not the premise. The exquisitely bored spend hours pondering the *how*. The idea is to find the connections you need, and circulate in the places where you can find others to help you to the next level.

More About The Exquisitely Bored

Back to *"who"* are the exquisitely bored. Let's delve into where they came from in the first place. They retired like everyone expected them to, whether it was because of age or because they sauntered up to the retirement bar with enough savings and investments to make it work. Others realized that having their health was a value and had a long-term plan for an early exit. Some were forced into retirement—ageism and a whole bunch of variables at play have left many folks with a sleep-in and an unplanned day.

Every person I've talked to who has retired has expressed a certain amount of negative sentiment about the transition. It's no wonder that, if you work in a routine for decades and then suddenly life opens up to your every whim there's going to be some trepidation about what's next. In most of the cases, there is no conversation about what's next. That's probably the biggest insight through all of this for myself, which makes me realize how unique the exquisitely bored are. The fact that yes, they are everywhere, but not like regular retired people *everywhere.* Retirement is a very "follow the herd" mentality. I've been in very few situations where I've even heard the notion of "finding what's next" be expressed. I've definitely heard the bragging rights of the people who retired on the younger side, and I've heard from the ones who miss what they did for a living. But where is the dialogue around a new term in life? A *what's next* mentality is not so prevalent. Your skills and talent after a full career in the workforce far exceed that of a younger, inexperienced worker. Do we, as an entity, lack confidence? Do we second guess our unique and individual gifts after being raised in a society of sheep herd mentality? Is it something subconscious from our political and socialized upbringing that sets us on such a mundane and preordained course? Can we start to explore *how to work* without going to work? Are we ingrained in the routine aspect of working *for the man,* going to a physical office and dreaming of the watch at the end of our 35-year career? The watch signifies the abrupt end to work life as we know it, and away we go to be old, pale and stale.

Living Longer

It's a fact that we are living longer. Have we prepared ourselves for 90 years? Or 100 years? How can there not be a *what's next* when at 60, one could potentially have 40 more years to get this life thing right! Think about 40 years and what that could look like in terms of the people you could influence, make money from, support and learn from. The notion of retirement age has been founded decades ago on an archaic and dated definition. The concept of it has barely been questioned let alone disrupted. Reports from the McKinsey Health Institute show that even though we are living longer, we are not in the best health. In 1948, the World Health Organization's founding con-stitution defined health as a "state of complete phys-ical, mental and social wellbeing and not merely the absence of disease or infirmity" (www.weforum.org). If this is the case, do we think that retirement is the best assurance of mental and social health? McKinsey further says this definition "recognizes the relevance and interdependencies of physical, mental, social, and spiritual dimensions," and that such a view should be the foundation of a new approach to healthier living.

Yet nothing has changed when it comes to shifting attitudes and age around retirement. We know that retirement can be a difficult transition for many and tied up in a variety of mixed emotions, both good and bad. What if we were to challenge the traditional and set aspirations earlier on for this phase of our life? What if we were to have a further, more in-depth understanding of the entire process and phases that make up retirement? Would that help us to make different decisions sooner? And perhaps hold us to a higher benchmark upon retirement, to transition to a new term that is more fulfilling and meaningful.

Key Takeaways:

The exquisitely bored embrace that there is no one linear path to the next life term, and they strive to answer the question: *What's next for me?*

The exquisitely bored have so much more to offer than a complete career halt at a certain age. The current culture limits creativity and the options for *what's next.* It's time for a shift that supports emotional and psychological evolution without the bounds of a systemic expectation.

Being exquisitely bored is about putting fulfillment ahead of survival. Yes, surviving and getting by is important, but thriving and finding fulfillment is imperative for meaningful exchanges and continuous learning.

Reflections:

Are you thinking about the retirement stage and worried? Are there areas of your skill set that you can consider carrying on into your later years?

Have you thought about retirement differently? Is this a new way for you to think about what retirement can be now that you see it as a systemic construct?

Do you subconsciously find that you group people and develop perceptions about them based on their age?

Finding Your Exquisitely Bored: Actions

1. Decide if you have an exquisitely bored trait, something that you are exceptional at.

2. Next, make a list of the skills that you developed throughout your work life that you feel you did exceptionally well. You can also make a list of all the things you feel come naturally to you.

3. Now, make a list of the things you are completely, utterly passionate about. It doesn't matter if you are good at them or have an in-depth knowledge of them. Write down what truly makes you happy when you see or experience things to do with that subject.

EXQUISITELY BORED BLESSINGS

"Often when you think you are at the end of something, you are at the beginning of something else."
– Fred Rogers

"Living each day as if it were your last doesn't mean your last day of retirement on a remote island. It means to live fully, authentically and spontaneously with nothing held back." – Jack Canfield

"Retire from work, but not from life." – M.K. Soni

"Don't simply retire from something; have something to retire to." – Harry Emerson Fosdick

"You are never too old to set a new goal or dream a new dream." – C.S. Lewis

"And in the end, it's not the years in your life that count. It's the life in your years." – Abraham Lincoln

"For many, retirement is a time for personal growth, which becomes the path to greater freedom."
– Robert Delamontague

....

"Retirement is not in my vocabulary. They aren't going to get rid of me that way." – Betty White

....

"Age is an issue of mind over matter. If you don't mind, it doesn't matter." – Mark Twain

....

"Do not grow old, no matter how long you live. Never cease to stand like curious children before the great mystery into which we were born." – Albert Einstein

....

"Don't act your age in retirement. Act like the inner young person you have always been." – J.A. West

....

"Retirement isn't the end of the road, but just a turn in the road." – Unknown

....

"I always likened retirement to falling off a cliff, and then you have to kind of brush yourself off. – Steve Young

....

"Courage is a special kind of knowledge: the knowledge of how to fear what ought to be feared and how not to fear what ought not to be feared."
– David Ben Gurion

....

"I love to take something ordinary and make it really special." – Ina Garten

....

"It is never too late to be what you might have been." – George Eliot

....

"Do the best you can until you know better. Then when you know better, do better." – Maya Angelou

....

CHAPTER 2
WHOSE IDEA WAS THIS?

"Unlearning 120 years of thinking should be easy; none of us were even alive."
– Exquisitely Bored

The premise of retirement was originally founded on government policy during the late 19th century and the 20th century. The Canadian physician, William Osler, gave a valedictory speech in 1905 to the John Hopkins Hospital. In his address he boldly stated that a man's best work was accomplished before he was 40 and that by 60 he should retire. He commented that the ages between 25 and 40 were the 15 golden years of plenty. Workers between ages 40 and 60 were tolerable because they were "merely uncreative". But after age 60 the average worker was useless and should be put out to pasture. Retirement pensions were also originally attached to life expectancy, and historically, tax laws are what incented employers to implement pension plans. We can start to realize that retirement is fast becoming an anachronism, something completely removed from its historical time which no longer serves the structure and work world realities of the current day.

By 1910, Florida got to be distinctly available as a retirement destination to the white collar class. Retirement communities started to show up in the 1920s and 30s. The explosion of golf courses and the onset of films and TV transformed having nothing to do into a leisure time activity. In 1955, Senior Citizen Magazine contained the first popular usage of the phrase "senior citizen." Advertising that encouraged freedom at age 55 didn't help the case either.

According to the Mental Health Foundation, one in five of retirees face depression, especially those who live alone. Physical health problems can also make people more vulnerable to mental health issues. Recent studies have indicated that "retirement increases the chances of suffering from clinical depression by around 40 percent, and of having at least one diagnosed physical illness by 60 percent." This is deeply disturbing data to read and realize. And yet very little has taken place to mitigate and manage a huge proportion of our population and guide them to a healthier, more positive approach to retirement. Also, when we think of those coming up through the ranks who are stressed about retirement, we need to start educating and mentoring accordingly so that they can instead be excited about a new life term and the deep fulfillment that can come with it. If they could see more options, more variety for how to approach this life phase, they would feel more prepared and could mobilize more effectively. For example, gradually moving towards it, knowing there are variations on job roles, hours worked, remote work considerations, new ways to learn and other variables, could mean an easier, less stressful transition. Perhaps the transition is taking courses and certifications while you still have one foot in a career but can prepare for the next term at the same time. This kind of bold, disruptive thinking is needed to provide a new frame of reference for retirement.

We need to perhaps consider that the definition of work has changed. When William Osler said what he did, he was likely referencing farmers and labourers, because running a farm after a certain age would have been limiting. We are no longer necessarily living in a time with the same concentration of physical labour type jobs. In fact, the school year is still modelled after the farming seasons, when farmhands could be in and out of learning environments and still run the family farm. If we look at our current world and the kind of roles and careers across various industries, we can quickly observe that the archaic definition of retirement is no longer relevant. So why are we subscribing to the same old-fashioned meaning of what retirement and age means? We haven't had a collective movement yet around disrupting retirement thinking and the industry as a whole. Are we ready for a retirement revolution to dispel an old way of thinking and behaving, and instead introduce a new era of doing, living and realizing potential?

Collective Change

Having made this transition myself towards what others would traditionally call retirement is what my husband and I refer to as being the new firebrands of what typical retirement is supposed to look like. It's not an old concept to us—we didn't have children either in a decade when society wasn't entirely ready to accept what that could look like for some. We were in our late 40s when we moved into our new life term. The traditionalists would say, "You retired much too young." However, if you see this now from the new, forward-looking perspective of retirement, we are in fact living examples of the movement I'm advocating for. Demonstrating the proof of concept has greatly clarified for me exactly how this can play out for others. It doesn't mean you don't experience the phases I describe in this book. The phases are still important to arrive at your greater meaning, fulfillment and new version of yourself.

The change of lifestyle, the change of priorities and the intersection of freedom is truly the foundation from which you can build your new life term. It is no different from how you prepared for your original career; it employs the same thinking, self-reflection and grit. But like all movements, the pioneers have the hardest path to evangelize, build, and incent change. The exquisitely bored that I know have likely had a more difficult time to stand in the face of commentary, defy societal expectations and unlearn over 120 years of systemic thinking. It's not easy to inspire widespread transformation as those drawn to counterculture tend to ask questions, resist the status quo and interrupt the way it's always been done. I'm looking for the exquisitely bored to mobilize, motivate, educate and support this powerful movement of change. With common purpose and a shared vision, this is a powerful group that can inform and implement collective change.

Key Takeaways:

The notion of retirement is an outdated term that does not apply to the majority of the working age of today's society.

We must change our thinking to break the pattern of what society has previously told us regarding when and how we must retire.

Retirement does not mean that you are unfit to continue working and learning. You can still achieve fulfillment after retirement.

Reflections:

Now that you understand how retirement came to be as a life phase, what other constructs come to mind that you may have been born into but are not yet aware of?

Are there ways you can start actively talking differently about retirement and the older generation? Can you start to change the dialogue in your own world to match a more modern way of thinking?

If you were given the opportunity to prepare for your retirement while you were still in your career, what would that look like for you? What kind of learnings and actions would you take to build towards something fulfilling in retirement?

Finding Your Exquisitely Bored: Actions

1. Take your list from the previous chapter and start distilling down what seems to be a common theme. Find the one or two themes that stand out more than the others.

2. Write down all the roles or initiatives connected to your themes that you think could earn you money.

3. List out one small action you could take towards making that a reality. It could be reading material, researching others doing the same or simply learning more on the topic.

EXQUISITELY BORED
BLESSINGS

"Since we cannot change reality, let us change the eyes which see reality." – Nikos Kazantzakis

....

"The only way to make sense out of change is to plunge into it, move with it, and join the dance."
– Alan Watts

....

"If there is no struggle, there is no progress."
– Frederick Douglass

....

"Sometimes if you want to see a change for the better, you have to take things into your own hands."
– Clint Eastwood

....

"They always say time changes things, but you actually have to change them yourself." – Andy Warhol

....

"If we don't change, we don't grow. If we don't grow, we aren't really living." – Gail Sheehy

....

"Change the changeable, accept the unchangeable, and remove yourself from the unacceptable."
– Denis Waitley

....

"Life is about not knowing, having to change, taking the moment and making the best of it, without knowing what's going to happen next." – Gilda Radner

....

"Change brings opportunity." – Nido Qubein

....

"Without change, something sleeps inside us, and seldom awakens. The sleeper must awaken."
– Frank Herbert

....

"The world hates change, yet it is the only thing that has brought progress." – Charles Kettering

....

"Action and reaction, ebb and flow, trial and error, change – this is the rhythm of living. Out of our over-confidence, fear; out of our fear, clearer vision, fresh hope. And out of hope, progress."
– Bruce Barton

....

"Life belongs to the living, and he who lives must be prepared for changes."
– Johann Wolfgang von Goethe

....

"Change is not only likely, it's inevitable."
– Barbara Sher

....

"If you feel like it's difficult to change, you will probably have a harder time succeeding." – Andrea Jung

....

"I try to contrast; life today is full of contrast...We have to change." – Gianni Versace

....

CHAPTER 3
STAY INTERESTED.
BE INTERESTING.

*"To pass food at interesting tables,
one must feel obligated to bring your own
plate of interesting."*
– Exquisitely Bored

Now that we know how retirement came to be and we know things won't change overnight, how do we navigate this world as we know it or expect it to be, even if we aren't quite there? Staying interesting and relevant is something that I discuss a lot with others. Working and continuing learning is one way to ensure we always have something to talk about that's unique to us as a person. This gives the outside world a glimpse into our personality, our reason for being and the character of our name and individuality. This is something we look for in others and one of the reasons why we gravitate to new people and form relationships. Why should we not feel the same pressure and expectation for ourselves?

If we can't bring interesting things and ideas to the tables we break bread at, then why should we be at those tables? Interesting people want to be in the presence of other interesting people. It stings a little to confront reality and ask ourselves: How interesting are we? If we aren't pursuing interests, hobbies, learning or setting expectations for ourselves, how can we develop and grow in new ways? Continuous learning expands our mindset, stretches our thinking and keeps us in the game of life. Grasping how long some of our lives may be adds a new perspective to how much time we may actually have. Time to sign up, join, create, build, learn and share. The exquisitely bored have an innate curiosity to see what they can accomplish. There is a negative driving the positive. It's often a drive to stay youthful and relevant. If the negative is energy and sparks the action, then it doesn't matter that it's coming from a negative place. It's like working out because you don't want to look like the person in the worst physical condition you know. Find your trigger and harness it. The pursuit of the cure can be a powerful motivating factor. This will be far more powerful and magnetic than the trade-off. Is it the fear of being like everyone else at a certain age? Is it the fear of becoming irrelevant and unnoticed in a room? Is it the fear of living like we are just taking up space instead of contributing? It should be. These are all justified fears and driving forces to incite us to action. Individuals living out their passions through creating and doing are optimizing their years, their strengths and their personal equity from a physical and mental place.

Pass It On

There is a company whose entire business model is based on older generations training and mentoring Generation Z. You don't get to be exquisitely bored and then have all your talent and knowledge base drop off. People need that intellectual capital and they are willing to pay for it. You've spent a lifetime building self-awareness, you've mastered the art of negotiating, you know how to build organizations, you've hired and fired, perhaps you have speaking skills and specific certifications, plus a multitude of other work-related skills. All of these talents are learned over time and gained with experience. Having mentors and leaders that can educate and support is crucial to our next generation making it.

Have you considered what you bring to the younger set? Your network, your intuition, your grit and resilience. Imparting these abilities to others means lending a different perspective and can be a game

changer for those struggling or starting out. Foster-
ing intergenerational relationships is crucial to gaining
insights to match the knowledge you are bringing to
the table. Should you just stay stuck in your generation of music? Books? Technical skills? Or should you
be learning as you are teaching? Bring your background in investment planning, financial management, business acumen and organizational structure
to someone embarking on a start-up. Think about
your ability to take practical business principles that
haven't changed, and match that to companies that
need your expertise. Where do we stand on confidence? Society sees it all as a downward slope, so I'm
guessing our confidence takes a beating and wanes
as we age. We don't see ourselves as having the same
impact or abilities. Do you realize though that youth
have been taught in this new generation to respect
and identify age as sage, as a positive? They can often
be more conscientious on the subject of ageism and
open to the possibility that everyone brings ideas to
the table. What should stop us then, if the new generation is already pre-disposed to treating us better than we treated our own peers in our past work
world? The mental health movement and easy parenting trend has actually handed us our *what's next*
on a platter. There are real advantages to mobilizing
for the new based on forward thinking and cultural
trends. We should be more than prepared to set forth

with our skills and determination to create, make and learn our new version.

See The Signs

Take time to think about what really ignited you to get up each morning. Where did you draw your energy and motivation from? Was it money, leading, organizing, creating, teaching? Whatever it was, that's your first clue. Your second clue is: What are the kinds of things you spend your time on, now that you are retired? Where do you see a large piece of your pie chart residing now that you have time for passion-fueled pastimes? The answer also lies in recognizing where you are focusing and being drawn to. The natural movement and gravitation to certain activities and things should be a prompt for what your exquisitely bored may be. I'm guessing those are the things you do well. They are the things you spend hours on, perfecting, researching, reading, doing and seeking. Is it a newfound creative outlet? Perhaps it's an area of volunteerism. Maybe it's built around service.

Whatever it is, take notice and see where you are focusing your time and attention. It will be the first step in identifying the area and skills you bring to the table for further exploration. Can you build something around this way in which you have started spending your time? Do you need to learn more skills to further develop this area? Can you monetize it? How would it feel for you to make money doing those things? If someone were to pay you for being good at those things, imagine that! It might be hard to picture at first. Passion and talent will be the driver, not money. The money will follow but it may or may not be your impetus. With self-reflection, once the inner revelation starts to unfold, it's going to be impossible to stop the process.

Unlimited Thinking

There is an arrogance of sorts to the exquisitely bored. They don't see themselves as not being useful. It doesn't cross their mind. They still struggle internally with confidence and all the *feelings.* But they don't actually imagine a world in which they don't succeed in some capacity. There has to be an arrogance and an attitudinal air of *I'm more than this.* That is the fire that feeds the discomfort of sitting in your inadequacy. Passion doesn't see something not working. It can see variations on the idea or the invention, it can be humble, but it doesn't take no for an answer. There is an innate confidence that everything is a matter of time. Things do have to meet up in a scenario of time and place. But the exquisitely bored believe that eventually there will be something of value, of interest, and that it will consist of skill and a drive to do something exceptional. In fact, it will become so thought-provoking that it will consume your every thought. What if you are, in fact, a retired visionary thinker? Your entrepreneurial spirit is not going away just because you retired. Nothing caps your potential more than a retired mindset.

Meant For More

Ego gets us in trouble. We've been taught that ego is bad, ego is puffed up pride, that it's not conducive to open-minded learning or working well with others. However, what if we could rein in our ego and use it to our advantage? Ego can be about understanding your motivations and harnessing success. In retirement, our confidence wanes and we feel more insecure about our approach to life. But if our ego tells us we were meant for more, then what is an age to stand in our way? Most people don't give a lot of thought in pre-retirement about how things will shape up when they reach their financial goals. It's difficult to have a growth mindset when everything we are taught about this life phase is the exact opposite. One thing I noticed about literature and research geared to the retirement audience is how childlike and basic in tone that it all seems to be. It speaks to retirees like they are children, and we all know that the 60-year-old of today is not the 60-year-old of yesterday. And an 80-year-old is not necessarily in the same frame of mind as a 65-year-old. But the retirement bucket has us all in a similar grouping and very little exists to support a different narrative than the same old story of what is supposed to happen when you are done working.

A Conscious Choice

The pre-planning for retirement should be more geared toward the goal of continuing meaningful work rather than the end to a long and storied career. Being self-aware enough to understand that there can be a lot of joy realized in work itself can mean that people work longer and enjoy a greater sense of purpose as they age. A reframing of retirement means that people could concentrate on the skills and talents that they most gravitate to. It's an amazing opportunity to focus on the work you enjoy. In turn, you bring something interesting into conversations. Some terms we are beginning to hear are second acts, encore careers, post-careers, and this is all much-needed reframing of the typical lingo we are so accustomed to hearing around retiring. It's different for everyone and highly personal, but we need to be able to talk about it in new ways and accept that a lot of us don't fit the traditional retirement mold.

There is more to plan for than just the financial piece. Money means different things to different people when they reach their financial retirement goals. It's difficult to find information and resources to do with the emotional and social challenges that present in retirement. Having a genuine and authentic social curiosity about the world around us and those we meet means we become more interesting to others. Part of the experience is making others feel that they are truly valued and heard. When these connections can be developed and nurtured, we automatically re-alize new perspectives and new ways to engage, and our own personal brand begins to form. The world around us has much to offer if we are only willing to dig a little deeper. A lot of this is basic paying atten-tion. By doing so, we learn, we communicate and we grow. Being interested in others is the direct route to being interesting to others.

Key Takeaways:

We are naturally more interesting as people when we are actively interested in others. By staying curious, asking questions and being engaged, we draw people in and in return become interesting ourselves.

There is already a move towards discovering your second act, your post-career or your encore career. People are realizing some of the emotional and social challenges of traditional retirement on top of financial ones.

The exquisitely bored become uncomfortable with the status quo and refuse to accept fixed thinking just because they are on a fixed income.

Reflections:

Are there interests and topics that you naturally gravitate to? Do these things or areas of specialty ignite a certain feeling in you? Is it a feeling of passion that energizes you?

Can you build something around these interests? Can you pause and self-reflect about where those interests might take you? Can you envision being paid to work on or producing something related to those interests?

What do you think would make you more interesting to others? Is there a goal or achievement that you have always wanted to work towards but haven't yet?

Finding Your Exquisitely Bored: Actions

1. Write down the names of the most interesting people you know.

2. List out the key attributes that make those people interesting to you.

3. Do any of those things match back to your own interests, passions and skills that you may have noted in the previous chapter exercises?

EXQUISITELY BORED BLESSINGS

"If you want to be interesting you have to be interested." – Austin Kleon

"Your life is your canvas, and you are the masterpiece. There are a million ways to be kind, amazing, fabulous, creative, bold, and interesting." – Kerli

"I'm curious. Period. I find everything interesting. Real life. Fake life. Objects. Flowers. Cats. But mostly people. If you keep your eyes open and your mind open, everything can be interesting." – Agnes Varda

"Develop interest in life as you see it; in people, things, literature, music – the world is so rich, simply throbbing with rich treasures, beautiful souls and interesting people. Forget yourself." – Henry Miller

"Trust that little voice in your head that says 'Wouldn't it be interesting if...'; And then do it." – Duane Michals

"Be interesting, be enthusiastic...and don't talk too much." – Norman Vincent Peale

"Never underestimate the power of dreams and the influence of the human spirit. We are all the same in this notion: The potential for greatness lives within each of us." –Wilma Rudolph

"Man's greatness lies in his power of thought."
–Blaise Pascal

"If we are to be really great people, we must strive in good faith to play a great part in the world. We cannot avoid meeting great issues. All that we can determine for ourselves is whether we shall meet them well or ill." –Theodore Roosevelt

"Man's greatness consists in his ability to do and the proper application of his powers to things needed to be done." –Frederick Douglass

"Creativity means believing you have greatness."
–Dr. Wayne W. Dyer

"There will never be 'the right time' in your life to do a great thing. You must create that time and greatness will follow." –John A. Passaro

"A dream becomes a goal when action is taken toward its achievement." – Bo Bennett

....

CHAPTER 4
DON'T BE A CLICHÉ.

"You are not the same as everyone else.
Why then, are you doing the same things
as everyone else?"
– Exquisitely Bored

Embrace your freedom intersection, be excited about what's ahead and take a break from the term that most likely held a lot of long hours, intense working situations, a myriad of work relationships and perhaps even work and personal life imbalance. It's okay to embrace the vacation feeling, the euphoria of finally living on your own terms. This will manifest differently for each person, but the phases you will go through once you reach retirement are consistently the same for a lot of people. In the meantime, do whatever you can not to be a retirement cliché. It's as I describe throughout the following pages: retirement wants us to be a certain type and demographic. The system is geared to segregate you and you must find ways to express your individuality, find your interests, your passions, and stick to your principles while doing so.

The Cliché Is The Easy Way

The stereotype is the easy way; it's falling prey to the things the system wants you to buy, what it wants you to look like, and most importantly, what all the other retirees are doing. Don't forget, you've been segregated into the retirement bucket. This has you hanging out with everyone your own age, being messaged to as an age group and a demographic, and being told you are too old and can't learn anymore. This leads to bad decisions about what to wear, not keeping up with pop culture, becoming uninteresting and irrelevant, and then the slippery slope into isolation, loneliness and feelings of unfulfillment. Finding your own personal identity, your own varied interests, and working to stay connected is paramount. It's the way forward for this entire term of your life and the very potential for the length of your existence relies on it. It's about adapting and staying true to your principles, passion and finding the people to make new things happen.

Connecting Intergenerationally

Intergenerational relationships are being seen in a

more positive light. The exchange of connections, knowledge and learning across generations is reducing barriers, promoting tolerance and building an appreciation for how we all bring something valuable to a room. Cultural differences play into this as well. When you are open to see outside of your own norms and biases, you open your mind to the new instead of the same old perceived batch of assumptions. It helps us build a collective awareness of what's happening in the broader world. Don't we want to expand our worlds in retirement? Isn't that why many retirees find reprieve in travel? Age segregation is a very real thing, and by volunteering and returning to work in some capacity we can overcome some of the actual societal structural barriers. If we never cross paths with other generations, how can we see personal growth, connect with new ideas and concepts or even stay in style? Is that why retirees generally start to all even look a certain way? Those shoes with those pants and the same sports?

I've noticed that retiree travel trends also seem to follow the same path. It's been made virtually impossible to stand out and have your own sense of character and personality. But if you don't even try to recognize it and disrupt the thinking around it, you will become lost in the sea of sameness and medical conversations. Birds of a feather do flock together unless you make a conscientious effort to rage against conformity. At least in some cultures, the older generation lives with the younger generation and the expectation to take care of your elders is present. This combination would even solve issues around housing, affordability in retirement and psychological chronic illness. The research and evidence supporting this is prevalent. In fact, the LA Times ran an article on "A Harvard Study of Adult Development, which began tracking more than 700 men in 1938 and continues today, found that older adults who invested in younger generations were 3 times more likely to be happy in their 70s than those who did not. They tend to be more alive, more alert and more optimistic about the future." My own personal growth has been about seeking what these connections can offer me and how I can benefit for my own learning, growth potential and even my business.

Be Bold Be Old

No one knows your age sitting behind a keyboard. The possibilities for remote work, building and creating a business, learning new skills and expanding your education are as limited as your thinking. And I'm not sure everyone cares as much about age as we think they do. I do think, though, that societal structure has normalized many negative thoughts and actions towards our aging population. It's time to start participating in changing the narrative to what the possibilities can be and defying the dialogue and roles that the system would have us adhere to. I believe the exquisitely bored are a group that are wired differently—they see beyond the limitations and they don't subscribe to what the person next to them is doing. Their dopamine hit is based around testing their limitations and overcoming prevailing stereotypes. When faced with the mortality of end of life, we have the luxury of nothing to lose. Can we not, ahead of all others, go fearlessly into the school halls, the pages of the internet, the textbooks of continuous learning and the closets of all things fashionable, to aspire to our personal best?

Identification Please

You never lose your identity. You just need to reframe it. Your identity may have been tied to a particular job or role, but it's always something you carry with you. Maybe you have always been a leader, perhaps a project manager, maybe a connector. Find ways to speak about what you did that are not directly tied to the profession. Learn to highlight the actual skills you built and the descriptions around those instead. These are the gold that will take you into your next term. One study, by Teresa M. Amabile at Harvard

Business School, asks a retiree in her book "Retiring: Creating a Life That Works For You", "Would you be more likely to say your work is what you do, or your work is who you are?" The retiree responded with, "Oh it's what I do. It's never defined me. I'm a human being, not a human doing." Sometimes gradually easing into retirement can give you the opportunity to work through and anticipate some of the identity triggers you may potentially face.

The Finally Fulfilled

When we do the hard work in The Quiet Mind and Still State phase, we can accept our new reality for what it is. Finding peace with that and doing the hard work of inner exploration and building awareness is part of the process we must embrace. With the Awakening phase comes acceptance, and the more humble we are to the uncomfortableness, the more we will attract what we need. The founding principle of heart-centred living is moving from head to heart. Once we get out of our own heads, we can quickly adapt through the shift and find alignment to where we see our focus being drawn to. Watch what you say and how you say it; are you adopting fixed thinking along with your fixed income? You were once paid for the value and skills you brought to the table; you are still able to offer that same value and attach it to something your passion and talent identifies with. Passion is what attracts the right people to you and it will provide clarity, motivation and creativity. Talent, on the other hand, is what comes naturally to you and once developed further can turn your ideas into tangible success. You can build on your talents until the day you die. Talents are grown and nurtured through further learning and expanding cognitive abilities. All of this is the recipe that the exquisitely bored have tapped into. This special demographic has income-generating power and they intend to unleash it. It is a mindset, a determination to live more fully, and to live a life full of deep meaning.

You are more original than a cliché. Discover your confidence to stand out and persevere. I think there is huge potential in the retirement pool not being tapped into. I see a lot of retirement clichés as I've been observing while writing this book. I wish I could say what I really think sometimes, but I'm not the authority on this topic—you are. At whatever age, you can mobilize to start planning for the whole other side of retirement. You can work it into your planning and have a sound understanding of how you intend to use your time when you reach your freedom intersection! You may still experience some of the phases, but future planning will mitigate the lost feelings and allow you to work through the complexities that will no doubt still arise. Whatever you do, be exquisitely bored, make it beautiful, make it bold and make it your best yet!

Key Takeaways:

Don't fall so easily into the trap set for you when it comes to the pre-set notion of retirement.

You have to actively seek to break the mold. To break that mold is to immerse yourself in cross generational relationships, technology and trends.

Your personal identity is not what you did for a living.

Reflections:

How can I stay current?

Are there clichés you can see about your own life?

Is there a way you can start interacting with different age groups other than your own?

Finding Your Exquisitely Bored: Actions

1. Write down all the things that people your age seem to be doing. Can you find a pattern of clichés?

2. Write down how you think you are different. Are there hobbies or interests that you have that seem to differ and stand out?

3. Can you find one or two clichés of your own that you can start challenging and breaking?

EXQUISITELY BORED
BLESSINGS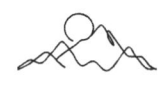

"Create your own visual style...let it be unique for yourself and yet identifiable for others."
– Orson Welles

....

"Attempting to get at truth means rejecting stereotypes and clichés." – Harold Evans

....

"Clichés are clichés because they are true."
– Harsha Bhogle

....

"Last, but not least, avoid clichés like the plague."
– William Safire

....

"There's a way forward by not relying on the old clichés." – Lee Evans

....

"People regurgitate the same old clichés and it becomes like a photocopy of a photocopy of something that's vaguely interesting." – Steve Coogan

....

"You have something unique that no one else has –
your life experience. That's the power of you."
– Mel Robbins

....

"There is a vitality, a life force, an energy, a quickening, that is translated through you into action, and
because there is only one of you in all time, this expression is unique." – Martha Graham

....

"Do you. Wear what you want to wear. Be an individual. Be unique and live your best life." – Kali Uchis

....

"Neuroscience is by far the most exciting branch of
science because the brain is the most fascinating object in the universe. Every human brain is different –
the brain makes each human unique and defines who
he or she is." – Stanley B. Prusiner

....

"A stereotype may be negative or positive, stereotypes present two problems: They are clichés, and
they present a human being as far more simple and
uniform than any human being actually is."
– Nancy Kress

....

"Cherish forever what makes you unique, 'cuz you're
really a yawn if it goes." – Bette Midler

....

"Being different means being unique and that's what makes the world an exciting place to be in."
– A. J. Odudu

....

"I think 'weird' is an interesting way to say 'unique'. It has a strange connotation, but weird is good. If you embrace your weirdness, you'll be on the way to becoming who you are." – Ben Falcone

....

CHAPTER 5
A PHASED APPROACH

"Phases are simply waves of change disguised as confusion and complexity."
– Exquisitely Bored

The phases that one moves through upon retirement are complex and rife with challenge. The following chapters outline the various stages that one is most often met with when it comes to understanding the intricacies of retired life. I see these phases more as insights that can help aid those who are not yet thinking of retirement, as well as those who find themselves lost and in a dark place searching for direction they didn't know they needed. It's these phases that very little information is offered on when it comes to retirement. We learn when to cash in our RRSPs, when to tuck more into our TFSA, and when to draw down more income, and conversations abound around the health of our portfolio in general. However, the emotional and social phases of retirement are left for us to figure out solo. When there aren't a lot of resources available or discussions around this, it makes it even more difficult to plan and know what's ahead.

There are a lot of emotions to process throughout the phases. Giving yourself time and space to feel all of it in an authentic and raw way is how you will best emerge on the other side where meaning and fulfillment await. Managing change is never easy. But retirement is all about how you choose to react to it. The choices in each phase are going to provide structure both from an emotional aspect as well as in your daily life. I also think that people don't want to admit their true feelings about retirement and this is why some of the phases I write about are crucial, namely A Quiet Mind and A Still State and the Awareness phase. This is where the ability to self-reflect and to be honest with oneself is imperative in order to find solutions for meaning and fulfillment.

Expectations

Society has long built retirement up to be the wonderful state of freedom and worry-free time in our lives. With this comes enormous pressure to meet the expectations head on and to have a fantastic experience just enjoying and being. However, we are not wired this way as humans. And if we are overachiev-

ers, we are definitely not wired to be content in a retired state. When everything about retirement speaks
to diminishing, it becomes difficult to match the expectations to reality. The entire atmosphere around
retirement is that of quitting, finality, mortality and
irrelevance. When we feel these looming realities,
but we were taught to expect something different,
we feel ungrateful and confused. We try to have grat-
itude, and as we work through the lifestyle adjust-
ments, it seems to become heavier. The expectations
of the reward phase are not equating, and alignment
feels entirely mixed up. You no longer belong anywhere specific and these shifts are deeply upsetting.
You start to feel irrelevant and uninteresting.

The important thing to keep in mind is that expectations are simply beliefs. Expectations are not reality.
We can change our mindset and our outlook and
take action. Let's understand that retirement is a
social construct. An article by the National Library of
Medicine outlines, "In some cultures, retirement is
purely based on the correlation to actual physical or
intellectual detriments whereas in the western world
it actually takes place for the healthy aged." The attitudes and beliefs of a society and culture can differ
regarding the value we attribute to people of a certain age. In some societies retirees are revered and
in some they are stripped of responsibilities. I think

there is comfort in understanding that, as a social construct, retirement is what we make it to be. Our culture imposes a certain expectation on us for age and role; however, we remain free to make our time and work what we need it to be for our own personal gain and satisfaction.

Judgement

It's natural to fear being judged by others. When we end up retired and don't often express the reality of our struggles, we are left sitting in fear of the judgement that comes from those around us. The only person who knows our true reality is ourselves. We may feel like others think we are ungrateful, that they think we went about it wrong, that we made a mistake, and you may feel like they are even judging some of the decisions that helped you get to retirement. The important thing is to believe your feelings. Have complete faith in what you are experiencing. As you continue through the subsequent phases in retirement, you are going to have to have an open and clear mind. There is going to be a little bit of a need for a thick skin! You are going to be making decisions and taking actions that lead to your heart alignment, and it will require a deep, solidified belief in oneself.

Personality

Everyone's personality and character are unique to them. Did you know that certain personality traits play a role in how people handle the changes that come with retirement? Studies have found that those with high extroversion tend to do better at adjusting. Perhaps they are able to talk more with others, have a larger support circle or are more deeply involved with extracurricular activities. Those who tend towards philanthropy, travel or expanding education may have an easier time or at least face fewer more complex challenges. Resilience must play a role as well. If we are accustomed to working through difficulties and have a high sense of self-awareness, then as we proceed through the phases, we may be able to navigate the realizations quicker. We may be able to reconcile our emotions faster and on a more profound level. Being open to new experiences is another personality trait that can benefit us in retirement. An innate sense of curiosity and adventure is helpful, as are understanding what motivates us and what strategies we use for coping with change and disruption. These are all variables affecting the different phases and how we will react to each. We could be conscientious when it comes to financially preparing for retirement, but perhaps we do not do well with change, which is why we are a planner to start with.

The fears and anxieties that come with change are then impactful for us and affect our transition. Our personalities can also change based on our circumstances. As our priorities shift in retirement and we develop different interests, this can help us adjust and acclimate to such a significant change.

A detailed look at the phases and what kind of emotions one can expect is helpful to realize you are not alone and that it's perfectly common to experience all or some of what I describe. One cannot possibly know what it feels like to be retired when it's a purely hypothetical thing. It's impossible to trust the process if someone has never explained it and you have zero insight into what to expect. I also think a lot of retired people won't admit to feeling lost for fear that admission means they made a mistake. There is no mistake in reaching your financial goals, no matter at what age. Yes, circumstances can change and people return to work for various reasons. But if we largely assume that the phases are about finding your new term in life and what that can be, then we can imagine the possibilities and the beautiful transition that can happen for many retirees.

Transitions To The Unknown

Moving into a transition, although challenging, can be

rewarding and empowering. Embracing the unknown doesn't need to be a terrible experience. Being lost is a time to self-reflect, build on your self-awareness and gain new learning about yourself. It's always uncomfortable, but retirement isn't the first time you will experience these feelings. Although it can feel compounded and overwhelming, especially as you age, if you use the transition time to build new opportunities, new interests and current strengths, you begin to see the way forward. Be present and keep an open mind for what's next. Your intuition is a powerful tool and it can take you where you need to be if you let it.

First Phase Freedom

As you read, you will discover the first phase, That Vacation Feeling, takes you to the extreme end of the phase spectrum. This first phase communicates that nothing is wrong and life is full of the euphoria that retirement brings! And you deserve to feel all of that! You worked hard to get where you are, and taking time to enjoy the rest and relief that it brings is important and very much a part of the process. It is a time of exploration, reconnecting with others and a flurry of social activity. Is the euphoria just simply recognizing the freedom of it? The freedom from the alarm clock and the constraints of your work day? The euphoria we can already see, from what I describe, is a temporary fix; it's a vacation and exactly that. Let's just say that what we don't know certainly doesn't hurt us in this phase!

Key Takeaways:

As you shift and move towards and through retirement you will experience phases. You will make choices in each phase that lead toward a more meaningful and fulfilled life.

Society has expectations for us. It's natural to feel judged throughout the process. Everyone is different in how they experience the phases and how they define fulfillment.

The phases will help you build more self-awareness. You will find new interests and you will continue to build on current strengths. Your intuition will be a powerful guide throughout the phases and retirement transition.

Reflections:

Can you think of another time in your life when you experienced great change that was also impactful? Can this help reassure you?

Can you find freedom in the fact that you are feeling lost? Can you tell yourself that it's okay to not have all the answers?

Can you have an open mind for whatever is next? Could this be the start of trusting that something wonderful can come from experiencing change?

Finding Your Exquisitely Bored: Actions

1. List out your personality traits that you think can best serve you for where your thinking is currently at.

2. List out your personality traits that you would like to develop further in order to build more resilience to change.

3. Each day, try to think of one area of your life that fulfills you. Try to focus on what about this particular area is meaningful and add it to your personality trait list. You will likely see a correlation!

EXQUISITELY BORED BLESSINGS

"Everything that is happening around me is very random. I am enjoying the phase, as the journey is far more enjoyable than the destination."
– Sushant Singh Rajput

....

"No serious–minded man should have time for the mediocre in any phase of his living."
– James Cash Penney

....

"I can't imagine not being in a phase where I'm trying to understand something or create something. That's the essence of life." – Kip Thorne

....

"If you knew that your life was merely a phase or short, short segment of your entire existence, how would you live? Knowing nothing 'real' was at risk, what would you do? You'd live a gigantic, bold, fun, dazzling life. You know you would. That's what the ghosts want us to do – all the exciting things they no longer can." – Chuck Palahniuk

....

"Every phase of my life hasn't always been perfect for me. I've had to go through some adversity."
– Quinn Cook

....

"There is a certain phase in the life of the aged when the warmth of the heart seems to increase in direct proportion with the years." – John Phillips Marquand

....

"It is a law in the universe that a wave of spiritual awakening is always followed by a period of doubting materialism, each phase is necessary in order that the spirit may receive equal development of heart and intellect without being carried too far in either direction." – Max Heindel

....

"Everyone's projecting onto you, or you feel like everyone is judging you. I feel like I'm being judged a lot of the time. You become really self–conscious."
– Kate Moss

....

"There are times when you're being judged on your appearance and you're not feeling your best self. It hurts, but as I always say, I try and be 100 percent myself all the time. So if I'm rejected, it just hurts that little bit less because at least I was myself."
– Adwoa Aboah

....

"People who judge others tell more about who they are, than who they judge." – Donald L. Hicks

....

"Most people who are criticizing and judging haven't even tried what you failed at." – David Goggins

....

"If someone isn't what others want them to be, the others become angry. Everyone seems to have a clear idea of how other people should lead their lives, but none about his or her own." – Paulo Coelho

....

CHAPTER 6
PHASE 1: THAT VACATION FEELING

*"I never met a Monday I didn't like once
I retired but Friday is still my favourite!"*
– Exquisitely Bored

You walk out of work. The taste of retirement cake is still on your lips, icing on the corners of your mouth. The euphoria is unmatched compared to many other life experiences. You can't imagine the alarm clock not dictating your every morning. What you can imagine is having a cocktail whenever you want, and random charcuterie boards on a Tuesday with friends, drink in hand. Every scenario has a drink in hand! It's like a permanent vacation but it's real life! The vacation is never-ending. Days and weeks go by, and your time belongs to only you. These days and weeks glide into months. You find yourself on a Monday driving one hour to try a certain kind of butter tart at a bakery. Tuesday back to that random charcuterie board with other retirees. Wednesday you make a day out of cleaning a closet. Your time is exclusively your own—

it's not hard to find idle tasks to watch the hours fly by. Even the mundane becomes exciting and new. You ride this newfound freedom train with pride and renewed energy. Reaching a financial goal like retirement is huge. It's something you have worked for, envisioned and manifested for years. This is the good life and nothing is going to stop you from doing whatever you want on whatever day!

The Inner Athlete Awakens

Finally, time presents the opportunity to discover or rediscover sport. You now have time to join a club, take some lessons, sign up for the men's or ladies' league and hit the course. Pickleball, tennis and bike riding are just a few of the ways you will pass each and every day once you have visited all the butter tart bakeries for miles around. This, my friend, will be the fulfilling trajectory that will set you on the path to retired greatness. Your game will flourish; you will find peace and satisfaction on every green, tee box and court. Insert any sport here and the sentiment around goal setting and earnest intentions are the same.

There's a BUT here. But what if it doesn't work this way for YOU? What if it's not enough? What if it's actually revealing more food for thought and it's starting to trouble you? All sports can be fantastic pastimes and ways to stay active. But sports are best when combined with a variety of other interests and hobbies to create a well-rounded retirement lifestyle. Diversity in a range of pastimes has been shown to drive mental engagement. Challenging the stereo-types helps to discover new ideas and perspectives. Overall well-being requires a variety of activities that support cognitive functionality, along with physical and mental health. And when not all of these needs are met, we start to challenge our sense of content-ment when we still see healthy years in front of us. For those years we want dynamic and fulfilling expe-riences. This is where the first seeds of doubt in the vacation phase start to plant themselves, but can still be ignored for some time.

Healing and Wellness

For many, the relief of having time to oneself brings healing. Many careers are extremely chaotic. They bring airports, time zones, living out of suitcases, tethered laptops with spotty internet, jet lag and the list goes on. Recovery is essential and retirement brings that ability to gain perception and awareness around what the human condition needs. The vaca-tion feeling stage often involves a focus on health and wellness. Being able to lose the frenzy took me the better part of three years. Your nervous system is not wired for some of the demands that careers now place on people. Some of you have punched clocks and stood in assembly lines. You have pushed papers, waited on tables, traded stocks or even driven for a living. You may not even know you are as creative and passionate as you are. There is a numbness that you have been programmed to accept. Days would have had rewarding moments, and those you have mentored, managed and promoted were meaningful interactions. However, the pressure of some roles has left many empty as they are fulfilled by bank accounts and bulging portfolios.

The vacation feeling stage is a shedding of the old and an embracing of living in the moment. You can suddenly entertain on any night of the week and the Sunday scaries have no power. They never really go away, do they?! This stage often entails purging. Homes are likely to be amalgamated and downsized, and work clothes will meet their untimely death in garbage bags headed to the thrift store. It is a busy stage as you can't turn down a social event or an opportunity to imbibe with other retirees. All the chatter is centred around building more storage for the things from the city house, getting rid of the things you no longer need, having the time to care for ailing parents finally, and rethinking how you use your spaces. Daily life no longer centres around the same routine. Workout regimens feel different now and perhaps are added to what had otherwise been a full calendar. Having the ability to focus on caring for one-self and suddenly realizing the joy of having an entire day devoted to self-care is pure elation. The routine opens up to a more loosely defined day. Some find themselves engaging in new house projects feeling a need to be busy and focused, while others plan travel and continue to celebrate the intersection of new-found freedom and the possibilities that come with it.

Preparing To Be Prepared

We spent our lives getting prepared for school. Lunch-es, outfits, science fair projects, after school sports and the dreaded parent teacher interviews. Prepa-ration had us then ready to enter the workforce. We had a sound understanding of deadlines, how to work well with others, and knowledge around balanc-ing household chores with a career, and some of you will have raised families. Preparation and opportunity worked in tandem to gift our lives with the fruits of our labour. Preparation is taught from the ground up. Guidance counsellors in school had the task of men-toring and directing us into careers we would excel at, parents and grandparents boasted about our abilities to their peers, and things became about preparing ourselves for the world at our doorstep. Work was all about preparation. Preparing briefs, proposals, statements of work, meeting notes and everything in between. When we arrived home we prepared dinner, we prepared for the next day, we prepared plans for the weekend ahead and we imparted the same plague of preparedness on to our children as per the cycle of how our world is structured. The systemic routine of preparing for work and reporting for duty.

To survive in this structured ideology is to define ourselves by what everyone else around us is doing. You get your standard number of weeks for vacation, you go on a trip where everyone else is going, you take your RV somewhere, you research a wine tour, you rent a cottage, you put the kids in camp and so on. In fact, in 2022, 45% of Canadians reported not using all of their vacation time. This to me would be indicative of the fact that people don't even know what to do with themselves outside of this cyclical, militant environment that breeds fear of the unknown and unpreparedness for having to face a reality of nothing to do. For Americans, it's 46%, further indicating that in North America we fail to understand what a life without work even looks like. No one in actuality prepares you not to work. It may be one of the least discussed topics when you really sit and think about it! We will talk later about how this non-dialogue about an equally long and vibrant part of our life is so unspoken of and yet acceptable.

It really is no surprise that we awake on retirement morning with no plan in place, no structured approach to what is now free time and certainly no preparedness around what it's like to lose all your peers. We take for granted how working with different generations, positions and personalities actually fills a gap in our lives with relevance, vibrancy and social skills. It can be true that some of you won't miss the overbearing manager, won't miss the needy hands-on management style that some teams command, and won't miss the bad work kitchen coffee that so needfully got us through each afternoon. But missing peers? That's a whole other level of loneliness that you won't expect in retirement. What starts to slowly happen in the first year of retirement is the grouping and categorization. No matter how young or old, you instantly become part of the retired demographic. You are grouped in with all retirees simply because you are retired! You are no longer relatable when it comes to your everyday friend circle if they haven't retired yet. The only other people with time on their hands like you are other retirees. It is a sudden departure from your world as you knew it. In this stage, it's fine though because you can't see past the euphoria of not having to work. You won't see the parts that start to slip away; it's a gradual process that takes hold, but you will notice later on. I think this is similar to the lottery winner. The euphoria is very real, but it's temporary. It's a positive change, like the honeymoon phase, but when rubber hits the road, the reality check hits hard. Nothing has prepared us to do nothing.

Special You

The vacation feeling stage is interesting as well, because only some will acknowledge your retirement accomplishment. Your act of getting to the so-called "finish" line holds a mirror up to others. It's an outright alert that they must be doing something wrong if they haven't met the same accomplishment. No doubt, your retirement announcement causes a flurry for a few financial advisors, as clients check in to understand where they are at on the retirement timeline. It will be interesting to see the ones who gift you a special bottle or even think of buying a congratulatory card. If you are on the younger side of retirement age, it's going to be even stranger to sit in a circle of lawn chairs while someone flips burgers and some of those around you who are older may not be retired. Be prepared for the segment who can't stand the sight of your retired, casual, relaxed self coming through the door!

The explanations with the gossip circles are also popular in this stage, as to how you made it happen. No one will want to give you the credit you deserve for whatever path you took. In the vacation feeling phase, things can be a bit sensitive for both the retiree and the observer. The retiree is taking count of those who are recognizing and sharing in their success, and observers are either tormented or willing to cheer for that accomplishment. It's hard to see the world where not everyone is sharing in the similar celebratory feeling, but it does exist and one might see that this is where the categorization starts to happen. The great separation of one from peers to the random Tuesday charcuterie board with drinks crowd. It's interesting how the segmentation of just being around other retired people is the only criteria for socialization. The whole *birds of a feather flock together* notion goes out the window in the sense that you may have absolutely nothing else in common with these new peers.

Relationship Complacency

Within this stage also lies the naivete around burning bridges and distancing yourself from the old work world and people you saw every day, which soon fade into the woodwork as distant memories from an old life. These are things you don't give a second thought to. You aren't self-aware yet to understand how imperative it will be to have kept and nurtured some of these relationships. When work has been so structured, we start to relate to people as only being part of our work world. When you strip all that away, the world becomes fairly black and white in terms of old and new worlds.

The new world comes with new peers, retired peers. So instead of nurturing and continuing to foster the relationships we had, we instead trade them for our newfound freedom world. When the work world literally forces us to connect and work alongside so many varying personality types, it's difficult to know the level of friendships we could potentially have had with certain co-workers. In most instances, we will have built bonds and connections with co-workers. Some connections meant work people overlapped into personal life. Dinners, after work drinks, introductions to spouses and partners, and even sharing family time. But how quick are we to ditch all of that and throw ourselves into the new retired people's world, some of whom we have absolutely nothing in common with. This happens when it's easier to migrate to those who can make plans with great flexibility and who are eager and willing to accompany you on road trips, shopping excursions mid-week and of course the Tuesday random charcuterie board with drinks. I guess it's human nature to migrate to what's easy. We become complacent in this cycle because the vacation feeling phase has low standards, no benchmark for curiosity, and we are easy to please in this phase. Riding the high is driving our every waking hour. No routine, no structure, no place to be. One shiny thing after another attracts our attention; we are all over the map with what charities we may consider working with, of course we'll volunteer, and there is an initial enthusiasm for pretty much anything. When you are seeing the world through rose-coloured glasses, it's hard to discern between the things that make more sense to give your attention to. I'm not sure we fully understand ourselves at this stage. It's a false sense of being.

When you no longer identify with your daily work world, you can imagine the profound effect that has on a person. Some people are working just for a pay cheque, and that's okay, but it's a world even less attached to our real passions and skills than we realize. Some people have not had the luxury of working in what they love or are passionate about. There are utility-based jobs that do a really great job of providing a pay cheque. And there can still be a sense of purpose derived from such roles. The reality of life is that food needs to make its way to the table, the kids need clothes and the car needs gas. Some haven't had a post-secondary education and some were not raised with tools and a support system. All of these factors play into the reality of the work world from which we end up retiring. The lens of retirement is going to be different for everyone based on socio-economic variables, but the challenges and discoveries will all be relatable in one form or another. This conscious awakening of seeing ourselves in a new light without a structured work day is just as jarring for the next person. The awakening and process by which we get to the phase of wanting more is similar in feeling and frustration for everyone as we move through all the phases.

That Friday Feeling

The length of the vacation phase, or honeymoon phase, is different for everyone. Like all things, the novelty wears off and minds wander in pursuit of the next dopamine hit that won't be nearly as prevalent in the subsequent phases. We initially think this is what we want our retirement life to be like. But over time, even the things experienced in the vacation phase become less exciting and spontaneous. If you think about the longevity of years spent practicing a daily routine, you can soon expect that without the same structured approach to our life and week, things will wane. My biggest learning and disappointment was losing a weekend routine. It wasn't apparent at the start, but over time I missed the build-up that started on Thursday and signalled to your brain that there were two special days approaching. Friday afternoons no longer felt the same because any and all days were like a Friday afternoon. Studies show that looking forward to something can be a mood booster. Friday afternoons seemed to put a bounce in our step and a fresh energy. Psychologically, we earned the weekend break and everything we experienced during the week was leading up to well-deserved time off. Fridays also embodied a group feeling, a collective sense of anticipation and joy for the weekend that everyone in the workplace and on social media would express. We cannot underestimate the power that Friday and the weekend held over our decades of routine-driven work and school life. Friday is a global feeling. Imagine, suddenly, the essence of Friday starts to disappear. It no longer holds the same significance that it once did.

This phase of retirement is also high enthusiasm. It literally sits at the extreme end of what I see to be the complete grid of all the retirement phases. I view this phase as a wild pendulum, erratically swinging through activities like travel, hobbies and sports, led by an overly enthusiastic social calendar. According to Statistics Canada, the remaining life expectancy for a 65-year-old male is 20 years and 22 years for a female. This means you will likely live ¼ of your life re-tired. How long do you think this vacation phase actually lasts? It's different for everyone and it's important to take the time to recognize your success in reaching the financial freedom intersection is well deserved.

The adrenalin rush of the vacation phase eventually subsides and you start to move towards a deeper connection with yourself and your new normal. I almost saw the vacation phase as dysfunctional when I look back in hindsight. But in no way do I want to diminish its meaningfulness and importance. It's part of the process and necessary to kick off the soul searching that you will do over the course of the next few phases.

Key Takeaways:

In the vacation feeling phase, you are experiencing euphoria. Everything is exciting and new. You feel like you want your entire life to be like this and you don't miss the structure that the work world provides.

A range of diverse activities in retirement is more beneficial than fixating on just one sport or one activity.

You start associating with other retired people regardless of common interests. You do not notice yet the subconscious segmentation that starts to take place. Peers who are still working may have mixed feelings about your retirement compared to where they are at.

Reflections:

Is there one thing in particular you are enjoying the most about being retired?

What kinds of activities are new for you in retirement? Who are some of the new people that you seem to be gravitating towards? And why do you think this is?

What are some of the new changes you are noticing right away?

Finding Your Exquisitely Bored: Actions

1. Make a note of which co-workers you are good friends with. Make a promise to yourself to stay connected and in communication with those friends so you can nurture and continue to benefit from those relationships.

2. Focus on 3 deliverables that can contribute to improving your lifestyle that will be easier to tackle in a phase where you have the energy and excitement to take on temporary initiatives. This could include moving, home organization and other more rudimentary changes that can help facilitate a new lifestyle.

3. Can you think of something to make Friday afternoon special so that you have a way to mark the weekend? Develop a Friday afternoon ritual that keeps Friday feeling different from the other week days.

EXQUISITELY BORED BLESSINGS

"Retirement: That's when you return from work one day and say, "Hi, Honey, I'm home — forever." – Gene Perret

"Retirement can and will be a glorious time in your life. You'll love the freedom and ability to try new things. It's a new phase of life; a chance to be a beginner again." – Richard Carlson

"The trouble with retirement is that you never get a day off." – Abe Lemons

"Retirement: a time to become much more than you have ever been." – Ernie J. Zelinski

"For retirement brings repose, and repose allows a kindly judgement of all things." – John Sharp Williams

"I'm not just retiring from the company, I'm also retiring from my stress, my commute, my alarm clock, and my iron." – Hartman Jule

....

"Retirement is when you stop living at work and start working at living." – Unknown

....

"Retirement: When you stop lying about your age and start lying around the house."
– Unknown wise person

....

"When a man retires and time is no longer a matter of urgent importance, his colleagues generally present him with a watch." – R.C. Sherriff

....

"I've been attending lots of seminars in my retirement. They're called naps." – Merri Brownworth

....

"Retirement takes all the meaning out of weekends."
– Unknown wise person

....

"Retirement: It's nice to get out of the rat race, but you have to learn to get along with less cheese."
– Gene Perret

....

"Don't play too much golf. Two rounds a day are plenty." – Harry Vardon

....

"In retirement, every day is Boss Day and every day is Employee Appreciation Day." – Anonymous

....

"In my retirement I go for a short swim at least once or twice every day. It's either that or buy a new golf ball." – Gene Perret

CHAPTER 7
PHASE 2: A QUIET MIND AND A STILL STATE

"May the still small voice speak volumes once you settle your heart and mind."
– Exquisitely Bored

Getting cozy is part of the quiet mind and still state phase. You've topped up the life pie chart with sports, family time, workouts, basket weaving and whatever else has struck your fancy. You are in a more settled state, and really trying this retirement thing on for size. I liken it to being on top of Mount Everest. You've arrived, you've accomplished the mission, the goal has a check mark beside it. This is where you think you actually want to be. Days are filled with a little more routine, although adjusting to a spontaneous lifestyle still has its challenges. You weave in and out of scheduled things to spend time on the frivolous things like planning dinner parties, art tours, stores you've always wanted to visit, things that you think are expanding your horizons. Volunteering makes an appearance, committee work, more dinner parties, picking fresh flowers for the bathroom, gardening and other mundane activities like sitting at friend's homes doing nothing.

This phase for me, in hindsight, holds an empty memory in that it was so entirely mundane that its nothingness barely registers. But at the time, you relax into life, feeling obligated to enjoy every second and remembering how paramount it is to be grateful. Glimmers appear in this phase; they are few and far between, but they are small indicators casting self-doubt and causing feelings of confusion. You continue to plan your way through each day to the best of your ability. Control emerges in many shapes and forms as you try to hang on to the structure that the typical work day provides. I noticed the over planning and coordinating of the smallest things in a subconscious way. This would be an attempt to build a routine, something faithful to follow that could be relied on for daily direction.

Existential Reflection

Gradually over time, the questions pile up. Since retirement is a significant life change and priorities have been reassessed, it's going to be natural to question why am I even here? And the age-old adage, what is the meaning of my life? This can be described as the seed of personal growth taking root. The mind finally has the time to be still and to ponder. Pondering to me is like puttering: It's mindless, relaxing and fruitful. Generally, when you are puttering you are picking up, organizing, cleaning and being active. Think of the mind doing the same exercise in the sense that it's organizing thoughts, picking up connections and seeking activity.

Settling the mind in this phase is necessary to invite in what biblically has been known as "the still small voice." Since I was raised religiously, I was taught that the "still small voice" cannot be heard amongst chaos or noise. Others may relate to this through meditation. How you receive signs and messages is personal, and across all belief systems the same theory applies: You cannot receive or hear your calling in a state of busy and uncontrolled distraction. The pendulum of being busy doing unfulfilled things will be swinging wildly as a result of the vacation phase. It's important to calm your spirit and arrive at a somewhat neutral state to truly understand the thought processes that need to happen. Readying your state for curious exploration is going to help you ask the big questions later on.

As you start relaxing into this phase, you will see

yourself beginning to search for a connection to something greater. Finding your passion and understanding what things truly bring you joy has likely been smothered by a busy and important work life. The elasticity of your mind is not accustomed yet to bending and stretching to the what ifs and the possibilities that lie ahead for yourself. It's important to build a state of awareness in order to receive your calling to your skill set, your passion, your joy, the things you are naturally good at. All this is easier said than done in what is the lead up to the most profound yet unsettling time of your life. If all you've ever been conditioned for is the cycle and structure of a career or general work life, how can you expect to transition without thoughts that provoke? If it takes 21 days to build a habit and you've been working one way for 20 or more years, how can you suddenly align with these new aspects of yourself?

Mortality As Emotion

All sorts of mortality assumptions are built into the financial side of retirement plans. How many years do I think I'll live for? Social security and pension plans are all part of the mortality calculator in the financial planner's office. But what about the emotive factor of how mortality plays into our existential self-reflection? I don't think it's a certain age. I think it's natural for people to want to leave a legacy. Mortality is tied to a sense of *have I fulfilled my legacy?* Will I be remembered for my principles, my passions, and the people I touched? There is a correlation between mortality and perception as we age. How we perceive aging is tied to our sense of meaning and purpose as we reach certain milestones. The challenge with our western notions around retirement and age is that the act of retirement pretty much triggers a deposit to our mortality mind bank. What greater signifier could there be than an actual retirement date?

I think retirement plays into the negative side of finite lifespan thinking and can contribute to fixed thinking that can be a tendency for retirees. My belief is that it incents comparison to youth and can be anxiety producing. However, when used as a way to re-evaluate our life priorities, I think a sense of mortality can drive us to act quickly. I associate it with rushing, and if mortality is what pushes someone to find their exquisitely bored sooner, then use that trigger to get it done! Can mortality, in fact, instead of causing us to look back on our life in the past tense, spur us forward to see what we can still create, produce and accomplish? If retirement connects us further to our mortality, can it then help us awaken to more authentic connections? Can we harness our mortality to build on this next term of our life? The flow of a quiet mind and still state is where we can ask these big questions and challenge ourselves around the kind of legacy we can expect from ourselves.

Connections And Interactions

The need for connection in this phase is interesting. Remember the *birds of a feather* we talked about previously? The broad group of other retirees who are all supposed to be your new besties? If you have this one thing in common, surely these friendships are destined to succeed. Your work peers are gone, some people relocate in retirement and take different paths. Peers were all part of the routine and the formality around those relationships worked effectively in the workplace. The psychology now of how you interact with people also changes. If some of you have been in business highly driven by client relationships, this departure from acquiescing to client's needs and wants is in the rear-view mirror. Meeting "important" people now takes on a different connotation. And here's the biggest insight, no one cares what you did for a living! Let that sink in. They will google your LinkedIn profile, but no one cares that you ran a bank, led massive teams of people, launched products or services, saved lives or dug ditches. This will be explored later on, but it's key to note that the quiet mind starts to figure this out. You begin to see your relevance slipping and sense of place and importance in the world declines. You can keep volunteering the information, all the great career accomplishments, all the wins, all the work travel stories, but the quiet mind starts to realize and notice the blank stares, and the conversation slowly veers back to golf scores. Don't go thinking golf scores matter—that's not where I'm going with this! This is about having more content for that LinkedIn profile they have googled!

I also think women are more likely to go unnoticed as I witnessed many inquiries to my husband as to "What is it that you worked at?" All the while I sat and waited to interrupt with my larger-than-life, minute-long, career elevator speech. As women, we are more likely to wilt on the vine and nothing highlights it more than being retired. With a cultural fixation on youth, women tend to become more vulnerable in retirement. Without the professional setting, women can often feel overlooked, and being an empty nester can also mean her social roles have changed. We worked hard to excel in the workplace, and lack of recognition can also play a part in finding new strengths and motivations to focus on. The premise of the exquisitely bored is to challenge the status quo and thinking. Spend some time in this phase contemplating the ways you can challenge conversation topics and ideas.

Enter self-reflection. You will feel ungrateful to be feeling this way. The quiet mind is taking this all in at this stage: observations are percolating and thought processes are streamlining. Nothing makes sense, and in a way it's like your heart starts breaking. It's not lining up, and only in a still state can you start to re-order your line of thinking and ask yourself the big questions. What those questions are I cannot say, as they are personal. Variables like insecurities, past trauma, life experience, age and socio-economic status all play into how the questions form and what your personal answers will be. The timeline is different for everyone because of these variables. What I can help with is assuring you that this is all a completely normal part of the process and all leading to your awakening! Your exquisitely bored revelation is happening and you will be rewarded with clarity in due time.

What's really important is that you are ready to receive the message. The inner reflection that is taking place is readying you for your quest for fulfillment. Continuous self-improvement, sense of purpose and meaningful contribution have long been hallmarks of a fulfilled life. Upon retiring it's normal to even experience depression. Work life always provided a sense of contentment for a job well done, personal growth and a sense of purpose. With this missing along with the structured work day, the lost feeling emerges. We begin to quiet ourselves naturally as an intensity takes hold. A quiet mind will be more conducive to finding clarity. Being able to discern emotions helps us receive direction and purpose in the awakening phase.

A State Of Mind

If we allowed ourselves this luxury of a focused mental state at a younger age throughout our career, we could align earlier and embrace the retirement process as part of lifelong learning. It would become part of our career planning instead of a stage in life that happens after we are done working. Imagine the benefit of not only a quiet mind but enhanced intuition that comes with youthfulness. With youthfulness we remain more open-minded to the possibilities. As we age, our mind loses elasticity and we become more rigid and stuck in our ways. We pursue the familiar and the safety net of how things traditionally unfold. Within our career tenure, we are drawn to the things we are naturally good at. Advancement and reward come with finding a path that plays to our innate skill set, and with hands-on experience, we find confidence and build an area of expertise for ourselves.

Often, people don't have the luxury of working in

something they are extremely passionate about, but everyone can still experience a sense of satisfaction and growth in their work life. If we allowed ourselves to explore this while working full time, we could map out a plan that work life segues into. It would allow us to be better prepared emotionally, financially and even in some cases physically. We could consider additional courses and education to build on our skill set, knowing that when we retire, we have built a plan that not only supports us financially but emotionally from a place of fulfillment. What good is all the money in the world for retirement if we don't feel fulfilled or a sense of accomplishment in our daily lives?

Living in the moment is sage advice. But so is planning ahead and anticipating a future that one has prepared for effectively. Earlier on we talked about living longer and how the notion of traditional retirement no longer exists. We have a long road ahead of many potentially productive years, so why should we not start planning ahead while we are still working? Should we dare to disrupt the notion that perhaps retirement goes away completely? There are certain jobs and roles that can't be done after a certain age, and physical ability can become limiting, but if we find other passions and interests, why can't we parlay our work life into an extension of our skill set? We need to change the dialogue around retirement. We need to instead reframe around what skill set someone brings to the table and not be influenced by age or other limiting factors.

Staying interesting and relevant in a room is the fountain of youth. It's not lotions and potions, although certainly when used in combination, potential for mistaken age can be a side effect! Some constructs we won't be able to combat—they are ingrained in society and that's okay. Instead, we can respond positively and with solutions. We can feel the power and confidence to shape our lives. How many self-help quotes exist around finding your "why" and sense of purpose? I tend to find this thinking limiting, and it puts enormous pressure on ourselves to have some sort of breakthrough, and more often than not, people connect this to money. I'm coming from a place of just people, not age, not household income, not gender, not anything but a personal desire to find fulfillment and a reasonable state of happiness in the *golden years.*

Do you realize the idiom *golden years* hearkens from the *golden age,* a reference indicating a time of great harmony and happiness that eventually became connected to the elderly? It refers to leisure time in retirement. But if we find so much confusion, lack of purpose and even depression upon retirement, does this not turn this Greek mythology reference into exactly that, a myth? In 1959, the Golden Years was an advertising campaign for America's first large-scale retirement community. I'm fairly certain a great many retirees will debate the golden years concept, at least the exquisitely bored demographic. The exquisitely bored are perpetually curious; they are driven and ambitious beyond societal norms. They have ideas, plans, inventions and the tools to create and manifest a new era. If society has all the expectations that it does for people's careers, then why not have expectations for retirement? Why not raise the bar and expect that people need to redefine this phase? Use your resources, use your talents and impart your skill set on others and your communities. We are in an era in which this demographic has financial resources in excess of any previous generation. When we look at the youth that could benefit from mentoring and we think of a 30-year career, one can only imagine the wisdom, advice and learning that could be shared and taught to the youth of today. Expectations are not a bad thing, and we need to hold ourselves to a higher calling.

From Head To Heart

If as the reader, you are familiar with heart living, you understand the importance of aligning with emotions, beliefs and your inner qualities rather than external pressures. The Quiet Mind and Still State phase are where compassion, patience and love reside. Once we establish this for ourselves, we can move from thinking into feeling. Retirement roads will take us deep into feeling, and that is where we can expect to move from a quiet mind and still state into the Awakening phase. Here is where we work on our prioritization of self and discover all of our unique personal abilities. It's where potential solutions and our personal story starts to build. We begin to have realizations founded on our principles and our belief system. Passion builds, and we start to attract the people we need to further align.

Key Takeaways:

In this phase you begin to struggle with the lack of a routine and as a result you may gravitate to behaviours and habits that aid in developing some semblance of structure around daily life.

Things start to calm down in this phase, and you have an easier time focusing and reflecting on where your life is at. You start to ask yourself big questions and begin contemplating what you can expect from yourself in retirement.

This phase moves thinking into feeling. You are faced with certain realizations.

Reflections:

If you are still working, can you figure out a way to segue that into retirement? Can you approach your *what's next* in phases?

Are there courses or learning you can accomplish while still working that allow for an encore career?

Is there a passion or dream job you have always considered that could be connected to your choices for retirement?

Finding Your Exquisitely Bored: Actions

1. What do you miss about having a routine? Start planning and adding the things that make your day feel more routine driven.

2. Set an alarm for each day to start rising at the same time.

3. Make a book list of reads that trigger reflection and self-awareness—books that can start to awaken and stimulate the synapses that have been distracted in the Vacation phase.

EXQUISITELY BORED
BLESSINGS

"A quiet mind cureth all." – Robert Burton

....

"Inner silence promotes clarity of mind; It makes us value the inner world; It trains us to go inside to the source of peace and inspiration when we are faced with problems and challenges." – Deepak Chopra

....

"If the mind falls asleep, awaken it. Then, if it starts wandering, make it quiet. If you reach the state where there is neither sleep nor movement of mind, stay still in that, the natural state." – Ramana Maharshi

....

"An inability to stay quiet is one of the most conspicuous failings of mankind." – Walter Bagehot

....

"Stay quiet, and you will enjoy the power of silence, stillness, and inner strength." – Ramez Sasson

....

"Everything that's created comes out of silence. Thoughts emerge from the nothingness of silence.

Words come out of the void. Your every essence emerged from emptiness. All creativity requires some stillness." – Wayne Dyer

"Silence is the great teacher, and to learn its lessons, you must pay attention to it. There is no substitute for the creative inspiration, knowledge, and stability that come from knowing how to contact your core of inner silence." – Deepak Chopra

"In the attitude of silence, the soul finds the path in a clearer light, and what is elusive and deceptive resolves itself into crystal clearness."
– Mahatma Gandhi

"Through the portals of silence, the healing sun of wisdom and peace will shine upon you."
– Paramahansa Yogananda

"The beauty of a lake reflects the beauty around it. When the mind is still, the beauty of the Self is seen reflected in it." – B.K.S. Iyengar

"Everything inside and around us wants to reflect itself in us. We don't have to go anywhere to obtain the truth. We only need to be still and things will reveal themselves in the still water of our heart."
– Nhat Hanh

"We can make our minds so like still water that beings gather about us that they may see, it may be, their own images, and so live for a moment with a clearer, perhaps even with a fiercer life because of our quiet."
– William Butler Yeats

....

"It is so rare to meet with a man outdoors who cherishes a worthy thought in his mind, which is independent of the labor of his hands. Behind every man's busy–ness there should be a level of undisturbed serenity and industry, as within the reef encircling a coral isle there is always an expanse of still water, where the depositions are going on which will finally raise it above the surface." – Henry David Thoreau

....

CHAPTER 8
PHASE 3: THE AWAKENING

"To suddenly understand the way forward with much clarity is to let your ego feel lonely."
- Exquisitely Bored

What is an awakening, exactly? It is when you come to a realization. This shift in perspective is often gradual, but it can be sudden. It's as scary as it is freeing. The exquisitely bored know full well the perfect storm that an awakening can create. This realization that you are meant for more will have taken you to a dark place first. But emerging is true heart living in action. You won't be able to see it any other way once you have the revelation for what's next. The actual shift comes later; in this phase it's about determining what I call the 3 Ps: your principles, your passions and your people.

Principles

Being guided by a belief is a principle. Find your principles. Is it the belief that you are meant to do more? Is it the belief that you are meant to give back? Is it a belief to be of service? Or, could it be a belief that you are meant to make a difference? Your principles are going to lead you to your passion. This is what will ultimately help you find your path. Your principles in a way are your moral compass. You've likely been raised with certain principles that you've carried into your work world. They are still the fundamental framework for being who you are. If you can match these to something you are passionate about, you'll start to feel the alignment. I'll take this opportunity to emphasize that it's okay to be a driver to make money. Not everyone has the privilege in retirement of endless financial means. In fact, when alignment happens, the money will follow. There are many exquisitely bored examples of money being the means by which a belief in oneself was re-ignited. When one is rewarded financially for trading passion and principles in work form, the incredible confidence and drive that can emerge is extremely powerful! Often, in retirement we cannot see ourselves outside of the career we did for so many years. We may not see ourselves as entrepreneurs or self-starters. Some things don't come as naturally for some people. But this phase is about finding what comes natural for you! Sure, the most logical direction is to go with something you did for a living, but the whole purpose is about finding what you gravitate to. You can act and find something similar or completely outside of what you knew for so many years. Your principles will provide direction, and once your actions align with your beliefs, therein lies your answer.

For me, the driving principle was being productive. Without feeling productive, I didn't have a north star directionally. If you can identify the guiding principle, you will have received the message. Self-awareness is a big part of this step. I had a grandmother who asked me every day after school what I'd done to be productive that day. It's no surprise that in finding my exquisitely bored, it would need to be something that felt personally productive. It would need to feel like I produced something for the world, or in my case now, for my clients.

Passions

Build your business around your passion. Business in this sense can mean many things, from volunteer work to work you receive payment for. Passion will be what you build each action around. For some, this is an opportunity to pursue things you were not able to in a career. Perhaps these were activities and skills you honed on weekends as hobbies, clubs, volunteer work and other avenues. How exciting is it, to take something you are entirely passionate about and now make money producing or servicing through that energy and skill set! Perhaps the passion is something you still need to learn to do which involves a course, lessons or some form of hands-on learning. This is the essence of the exquisitely bored! They find the thing they are really exceptionally good at, the thing that drives them every day that they now are able to explore more in depth.

When passion and principles are engaged, it's going to be difficult to stop the positive process that will begin to take place. It's important to note that passion can motivate and energize; however, it may not completely translate to mastery. Learning and building aptitude for something you are passionate about is often part of the process. Some of the exquisitely bored never stop working—they are still engaged fully in what they consider to be their life work. They are as much an audience for this as anyone else. Remember, quitting your job to retire is something that has become a societal norm; it should not be a guiding principle if someone is still enjoying and leading great things at work. We should not be socialized into retirement, and instead the shaping of all our years over a lifetime should be considered as a whole.

Perhaps your passion is a gap you have identified, a need. And again, I think that money can drive people to be passionate about certain things as well. If you are good at something and money is your driver, I don't think you can overanalyze the exact order of things. The idea for the Awakening phase is to find something you can offer to the world that fulfills your spirit. I think it's even better if you can get paid for this. You will have an alternate retirement income stream and people are happy to pay for value. There are some incredibly ambitious and exquisitely bored people building some amazing companies and creating incredible works of art, products and services.

People

Don't we always hear how important it is to find your people? In the Awakening phase, you will need to find your people to come along for the ride. As much as you need them, they are also going to benefit from the drive and energy you are bringing to the party! This will be one of the most rewarding discoveries, to think you can contribute and influence based on your vast past learnings. People are looking for this and need this expertise. The youth today need mentoring. You have built years of learning, decades of trying things and making mistakes. Imparting this to others and working alongside a team is going to bring you so much joy. With the Awakening phase comes the access to people who can make your efforts a reality. People will feel your energy, the shift starts to happen and the right people will present themselves at the right time. You are making it happen, and know that the laws of attraction are a very real thing. You will also be made more aware in this phase about which people are not your go-to. Not everyone is going to be a fan of your success, and keeping your intentions to yourself is the best approach until you can fully define where it is you are headed.

I've always been a believer that other people's energy can mess with your own, and when you are pulling away from the pack, you will be surprised at who stays around to support and those who don't. The exquisitely bored are not everyone, you are special, you have humbled your ego to embrace more. You have more to gain and more to feel in a deeper, more meaningful way. Staying interesting and relevant is a key driver for many, and there will always be those who aren't driven by the same things. Finding purpose and fulfillment involves intense self-discovery, and some people are not equipped for the work required for personal growth. Just because you are all retired in the same room does not mean everyone will equally find their sense of purpose and relevance. Or want to. Some are not interested and we cannot judge the path of another. What we can do is use our own gifts and abilities to speak love, acceptance and patience to others.

The Doing

The Awakening also involves doing. Creating, ideating, word of mouth, selling, communicating and finding the ways to share your talents and skill set. When you are ready to tell others, and again, I recommend doing this at the later stage so you can focus inwardly and accomplish what you need to without outside influences, you will be excited. Emotions are heightened, and it's euphoric to pursue your thing. Heart alignment is all about emotion in a trained and steady manner, and once you are awakened to what this new direction is, it will be hard to be silent. This is where finding your people in context of what you need help with is vital. The people you will work with in this stage will be meant to help you. Share your story when you are ready, because these are the people providing the tools for you to get started. Find someone to build your website. Find someone to brand your business. When they hear your story, they light up, and you in turn spark their creative process to produce the best results for you. Being buoyed by others in business during this time is essential for getting you where you need to be. Hanging your shingle may require business expertise from several areas, so don't be afraid to reach out and tap into your network or ask others to make a connection for you.

Marketing your business is part of putting your message out into the world. You will be surprised at how many people respond so positively to the exquisitely bored. We strike a chord with people, and in our humble act of leaving our ego behind, we can mentor others about the need for and importance of what work life can morph into. Communicating and evangelizing this new perspective is truly eye opening. Most people have not heard this angle before, and those who are still working need to hear about your experience. They need to be reassured that if for financial reasons they have to work longer, that's okay, and that is the best path regardless, for more reasons than they know! If you are imparting this learning to them about fulfillment and finding relevance, it's a way for them to learn to relax into their path and find a softer landing than others.

Self-Hope

The Awakening is realization, and it's about taking action. It's about no longer being able to stay still. You have become uncomfortable with accepting the way forward as it once was. Your open mind and curious spirit has led you to plan and action. Your inside voice is guiding you to fulfillment and authentic heart living. Your perspective has shifted and your intuition has told you there is more. Trust it. Instead of self-help, think in terms of self-hope: believing in yourself and knowing you can create and design a life around your principles, passions and other exceptional people. Your awareness and personal transformation will change your life drastically. You won't recognize yourself on the other side, and the emptiness will fade. The Still State prepares you and The Awakening has armed you for The Shift. The Shift is the most difficult of the phases but is essential to find your meaning and return to your true self.

Key Takeaways:

You are realizing something is missing. You feel a revelation towards wanting more.

You start to align with the three Ps: principles, passion and people.

The Awakening is about taking action: finding your *what's next* and implementing the steps to find more clarity around what you need in your life.

Reflections:

What is the belief you are most moved by? Is it to give back? Is it to create something? Is it to move towards an encore career?

Finding Your Exquisitely Bored: Actions

1. Revisit your list from Chapter 1 where you identified your passions. Decide which of these is going to receive your focus. Or it could be where your talent lies that you could be monetarily rewarded for.

2. List out how you can monetize this passion or talent and attach a framework to it that out-

lines what you require for implementation.

3. Make a list of the people you will need. Gather costs and next steps to move forward. This could involve updating a resume, creating business cards or planning networking meet-ups.

EXQUISITELY BORED BLESSINGS

"The millions are awake enough for physical labor; but only one in a million is awake enough for effective intellectual exertion, only one in a hundred million to a poetic or divine life. To be awake is to be alive. We must learn to reawaken and keep ourselves awake, not by mechanical means, but by an infinite expectation of the dawn." – Ralph Waldo Trine

"I've continued to recognize the power individuals have to change virtually anything and everything in their lives in an instant. I've learned that the resources we need to turn our dreams into reality are within us, merely waiting for the day when we decide to wake up and claim our birthright." – Anthony Robbins

"Waking up to who you are requires letting go of who you imagine yourself to be." – Alan Watts

"Like the elephant, we are unconscious of our own strength. When it comes to understanding the power we have to make a difference in our own lives, we might as well be asleep. If you want to make your dreams come true, wake up. Wake up to your own strength. Wake up to the role you play in your own destiny. Wake up to the power you have to choose what you think, do, and say." – Keith Ellis

....

"Once the soul awakens, the search begins and you can never go back. From then on, you are inflamed with a special longing that will never again let you linger in the lowlands of complacency and partial fulfillment. The eternal makes you urgent. You are loath to let compromise or the threat of danger hold you back from striving toward the summit of fulfillment." – John O'Donohue (Anam Cara: A Book of Celtic Wisdom)

....

"There are three constants in life...change, choice and principles." – Stephen Covey

....

"Change your opinions, keep to your principles; change your leaves, keep intact your roots." – Victor Hugo

....

"Principles are the basis for developing a vision and value system for all." – Stephen Covey

....

"Important principles may, and must, be inflexible."

– Abraham Lincoln

"Great ambition is the passion of a great character. Those endowed with it may perform very good or very bad acts. It all depends on the principles which direct them." – Napoleon Bonaparte

"Strive not to be a success, but rather to be of value." – Albert Einstein

"Take courage and work on. Patience and steady work – this is the only way. Go on; remember – patience and purity and courage and steady work…So long as you are pure, and true to your principles, you will never fail." – Swami Vivekananda

CHAPTER 9
PHASE 4: ACCEPTANCE

"Ah the sweet peace of acceptance, knowing you can no longer be affected."
- Exquisitely Bored

The Acceptance phase is difficult and can actually be sad. Some retirees often feel depression and report feeling lost and directionless. But there lies great peace in any kind of acceptance that we may experience in life, and this is not unlike that familiar feeling. For many, your new reality is not what you thought it would be. It's a highly personal experience fraught with feelings of confusion, anxiety and even aspects of grief. You've left or are about to leave an entire life of peers, knowledge base, environment and routine. Adjusting to this phase is difficult, and even more so is having to accept that retirement doesn't feel right can be scary, jarring and overwhelming. In the Acceptance phase, it's helpful to focus on the fact you have reached financial freedom. You can experience life on your own terms now. Accepting that this can be a time of enriched learning about yourself, a time to pursue your passions and interests, and better yet without an alarm clock! The more we prepare for retirement, the more of an exciting and positive experience it can be.

The issue I see is there is a wealth of financial preparation in the way of tools and resources, and planners and banks are all too willing to aid with a retirement plan. But there is very little available in the way of preparing emotionally and socially for this phase of life. If we could have a line of sight in our 30s and 40s to what retirement can look like outside of financial planning, we would be better able to assess how and when we approach our slow-down from the traditional work world. What if we could assess our path as a whole and identify opportunities for jobs we could gradually shift to in our second term of life? I see my network already doing this and I know it's a growing trend. It can certainly make the Acceptance stage easier and provide us with more control around making the transition.

Loss Of Identity

For an entire career you have related to your peers, to your area of expertise and your daily schedule with a fully structured lifestyle. If you worked for the weekend, even your downtime has been tied to your work regimen. In marketing we learned that the "back to school" September sentiment never goes away even long into adulthood. We carry the anxiety and feeling around returning to the school year despite our age. Systemic habits of this nature are deeply rooted in how our society is structured around seasonal marketing activity. If we have worked for decades, then those feelings attached to work are not going to disappear quickly and maybe never will. The sense of loss and not understanding who we are anymore is completely normal. How we currently view this as a society and prepare people for retirement, though, should not be normal. This needs to be thought disrupted because we could be spending a very long span of time in our retirement phase. Web MD reports that "1 in 3 retirees feel depressed, a rate higher than that of the adult population overall." If you were in a leadership position, your sense of loss tied to your ego will be even more profound. You no longer identify with "what" you were but now "who" you are.

It's also interesting how being without a title or work role identity leaves you without a point of reference in a sea of other retirees. Your sense of self-importance and placement in the order of things feels off its axis. Relating to your work world even comes with a host of feelings, biases and innate behaviours that were learned and became part of your persona over the years. Feelings of frenzy perhaps, needing the dopamine highs of winning sales pitches, celebrating wins, and even the particular behaviours of work peers. All of this combined formed your view of the world that you either thrived in or barely survived, depending on your work environment. Now imagine it gone and a new view for how to see the world and experience people, places and things is a complete departure from what you've known. Many variables play into the layers that contribute to a loss of work identity. Gender, age, work title, sector, co-workers, profession and the list goes on. In an era of always being "on" and tethered to technology, chances are, we absolutely identify with our work.

Beyond Work

Finding acceptance beyond work is your new normal. Adapting takes time, but for some by the time they reach the next phase that I call The Shift, they already know they are reaching for something more and acceptance turns to intent. But first there has to be a receiving of the peace that can come with acceptance. Accepting that this is your new normal and identifying the positives that can be felt as part of the journey. After awakening to what you are on the path toward, you can be at peace knowing that action will follow. But you cannot take action until you fully move through acceptance. Acceptance is a choice you make to know you can see things with clarity and a conscious view of a way forward. You want to see the world in its very realness without perceptions or your side of the story. It's important to truly connect with the present and find alignment. If we can remove emotion and over-thinking, we can start to assemble a new personal construct and prepare ourselves for what can be incredibly transformative!

Preparing For Action

You can still accept the situation for what it is and at the same time want more! This is the exact mindset to take into the next phase. Gearing up for shifting your thoughts into action is not only exciting but empowering. Action and change come from acceptance, and this is where personal growth starts to take root. Having a desire to improve, to build upon skills and to expand your perspective is coming to fruition as you move through this phase with calm awareness. The exquisitely bored want more, and your drive to explore the what ifs and the possibility of more will pull you toward where you now start focusing your energy. What if, in acceptance and having clarity, you actually start to build something really incredible? What if you actually find your alignment to what's next, quickly, and you accomplish things you never thought possible? In the next phase of The Shift, you will find that things move quickly. A sense of urgency prevails, and the sooner you move through the Acceptance phase intentionally, the sooner you can tap into the resources you need to move toward action.

Key Takeaways:

Retirement does not feel right for you. You accept that you are not fulfilled and that something more meaningful is required, involving change.

You feel lost in a sea of other retirees without a point of reference as your identity was tied to your work role and responsibilities.

You accept the situation for what it is but at the same time you can still want more. You feel a sense of urgency to take action and explore your options. With acceptance you find peace and clarity.

Reflections:

What about the work world was enjoyable for you? Was it the routine? Was it the consistent learning opportunities?

What attributes tied to your work role appeal to you in your second phase? Is it sales? Is it working with clients? Is it running the numbers? Is it creative thinking? Is it doing things on your own terms?

Can you take comfort in the fact that you are already acting on your convictions? You have been on a journey of self-reflection and certain insights about yourself have emerged. Can you feel your confidence building?

Finding Your Exquisitely Bored: Actions

1. If you haven't already, connect with a mentor for the coaching you need to refine and shift some of your actions.

2. Make a list at the end of each day that you treat like a work "to-do" list.

3. Form behaviours and patterns that mimic the work world you would like to see emerge.

EXQUISITELY BORED BLESSINGS

"The keys to patience are acceptance and faith. Accept things as they are, and look realistically at the world around you. Have faith in yourself and in the direction you have chosen." – Ralph Marston

"Acceptance doesn't mean resignation; it means understanding that something is what it is and that there's got to be a way through it." – Michael J. Fox

"Happiness can exist only in acceptance."
– George Orwell

"The first step toward change is awareness. The second step is acceptance." – Nathaniel Branden

"Serenity comes when you trade expectations for acceptance." – Gautama Buddha

"Surrender is the inner transition from resistance to acceptance, from no to yes." – Eckhart Tolle

"We must accept life for what it actually is – a challenge to our quality without which we should never know of what stuff we are made, or grow to our full stature." – Robert Louis Stevenson

....

"If I could define enlightenment briefly, I would say it is 'the quiet acceptance of what is'." – Wayne Dyer

....

"Once we accept our limits, we go beyond them."
– Albert Einstein

....

"Trust yourself. Create the kind of self that you will be happy to live with all your life. Make the most of yourself by fanning the tiny, inner sparks of possibility into flames of achievement." – Golda Meir

....

"Anything in life that we don't accept will simply make trouble for us until we make peace with it."
– Shakti Gawain

....

"Mindfulness is the aware, balanced acceptance of present experience. It isn't more complicated than that." – Sylvia Boorstein

....

"The only way to make sense out of change is to plunge into it, move with it, and join the dance."
– Alan Watts

....

"The acceptance of certain realities doesn't preclude idealism. It can lead to certain breakthroughs."
– Rem Koolhaas

CHAPTER 10
PHASE 5: THE SHIFT

*"Enter darkness, I see through you,
you are but a fickle and temporary thing that
wants me dead or alive."*
– Exquisitely Bored

The shift is exactly that. Your entire universe and life
as you know it starts shifting according to where your
newfound energy lies and where you want to go.
The shift can be full of uncertainty and is not always
planned. I struggled greatly during the shift, so much
so that seeing the joy some days was completely impossible. This phase can be a lonely and dark place
to reside as it is where self-assessment and extreme
personal growth occurs. Your desire for a different future is driving all of your emotions, and it's important
to keep accepting the change as it unfolds. There is an
element of excitement, but it's mostly fear and sad-
ness. You will no longer feel that some of the same
things and people serve you. Others subconsciously
feel you shifting and pick up on this transition. Your

frequency is not going to match the old ways. This span of time I think is dependent on how many years of untangling from the old life you have to do. If you have spent time already in the retirement space, you will have developed friends, routines, habits and thinking that require undoing. Most of these are not going to serve you in the new. It's the reality check, and there isn't one exact way to go about it. Shifting away from people in particular doesn't have to mean something is wrong. I learned that my shifts away from people were temporary. I didn't feel that at the time. I also didn't understand if what I was doing was wrong and if I was going to lose friends. But it was essential for my growth and state of mind. I was in a dark place and The Shift helped me find focus around what I needed to do to take action in my life. I also didn't want to talk about my changes and felt that my process was deeply personal. My energy and efforts were something I wanted to keep close to my own centre, and the disengagement was the right thing for me at the time.

Setting the Boundaries

This phase involves the death of certain ideas and things you thought were going to be more permanent. Most will not be what serves you and the untangling is extremely cumbersome. I'm a big believer in the energy that you emit and the energy that you receive from others. In this stage I wasn't yet attracting the energy I needed for clarity. I just knew based on my intuition that I was headed in a new direction.

The more you begin to separate from your previous version of you, the more tension you will feel. Tension from others, emotional tension, tension of your energy and a discomfort as you work through receiving the tension. The more you remain open to loving the process and the more tension you lean into, the more empowered you become. This is about setting boundaries, and others will see and feel you becoming unavailable. But in order to become the most powerful version of yourself, you will need to focus on the new self that is emerging. The more work you do to move forward in connecting with your principles and passion, the more the right people will appear. To draw strength, remember, you made the retirement happen, it wasn't luck, it wasn't coincidence, you made that happen with your hard work and goal setting. Therefore, you are entitled to every feeling when The Shift starts happening. Own it, feel it and dig in.

Behind the boundaries you have set for yourself, be busy. Start moving towards the passion and the things that drive you. Finding your exquisitely bored is your priority. Whether it's starting a business, volunteering or learning, the process of getting set up can be all-consuming. This is also where we start to feel energized. The more we accept the tension, the more we start to enjoy it. You will likely start to talk about your new business, new initiative, and new direction with those around you. This can make this phase even more difficult because not everyone will be respectful of your boundaries or receptive to your shift. The people who are comfortable in their own frame will be supportive and may even become part of your network. Some will not be interested and will separate. But the ones who are meant to be part of the best version of yourself will cheer, clap and show interest.

Find Your Mentors

Finding a mentor is an ideal way to build a support network. A mentor helped me with things like identifying value for my business, reviewing my business value proposition and helping to match my energy as I came into my power. I also found encouragement from the people around me who were participating in getting my initiative off the ground. From the person printing my business cards to my graphic designer, their energy reciprocated. There will be a genuine connection as the universe matches you with those required to facilitate and assist with your shift. Trusted individuals, partners and family members can help remind you of your strengths. Validation is helpful and affirms your direction as you further align with your principles and passion.

The Harder the Better

The shift presents another difficult force field in that the tension sometimes manifests like a magnet pulling you back into your previous habits, people and places. It's hard to tell yourself that you are on a separate mission and those habits, people and places are not necessarily a negative thing long-term. In the short term, they can complicate your energy, and I remember feeling frustrated and misunderstood. Some will go as far as to tell you not to work too hard, interfering with your personal tasks and goals, bullying into your calendar, and projecting other negative forces. "To everyone and everything there is a season." The people and things that served me previously all helped to get me where I am now in more of an indirect way. It's less judgemental to see it that way but that will be difficult at first for some of you.

Your shift is deeply personal. No one else is dialed into your plan like you are. The Shift can be full of shadows and it's where the real work happens. The Shift is best served by swiftness. You don't have to have all the details defined. As long as you are moving towards the ideal, you will receive clarity. As you have meaningful engagements based on your goals, you will be further fueled towards transformation. Confidence can also mean doing it scared. This stage will take you places you never thought you could go.

The following challenges help describe the smaller phases within The Shift that one may experience:

Challenge One – Dedicating Time to the New

This stage is where you need to be focused on what you have realized your exquisitely bored is. It will feel near impossible to give it the time and attention you want because remember, perhaps you are still untangling from the old! Find what time of day you work the best, when you are best tapped into your creative self. Keep the boundaries alive and well. They are going to be up for a long while. Having your head down and unwavering focus on what you see ahead is crucial for progress. Treat your day like a work day if need be. Revert back to your comfort level of a structured day and treat each deliverable like it's part of a work to-do list. If you are acting like you are working, then you are going to attract the same actions from others. This is where you can establish a routine and begin to see a more structured lifestyle emerge.

Challenge Two – Beginning the Untangling

Untangling from regular work life and an old routine or untangling from the previous version of you will all take focus and a plan. Gradually organize yourself with tasks that can be accomplished in short sprints. Set yourself up to see progress that moves you forward and away from what you once knew and the things that don't expand your world. Flat out quitting boards, groups, clubs, and anything that doesn't serve the new is part of the process to align with your goals. Saying "no" is a big part of this challenge. This is where hiding behind text messaging never felt so good! Polite, short messages that directly convey your answers and refusals mean your time is freed up and your world can open further to your new objectives.

Challenge Three – Outlasting the Commentary

People can be hurtful, and not everyone has the decorum to say the right things at the right time. I had to grow a thick skin as the haters are going to hate. They may be insecure about their own shortcomings, perhaps highlighting your spirit of courage and vision which can be much different from the next person. Everyone finds fulfillment in varying ways and no one should stand in judgement. Regarding commentary, my world was literally split down the middle. The new people, clients and supporters were believing in me and expressing their excitement, and the old was challenging me with negative connotations and limited thinking. Then there was the group who weren't even listening, completely oblivious to the long hours, energy and work I was putting into Exquisitely Bored as a company. There will always be the yin and yang of opposite forces, forming the duality to create enough balance for you to be both fueled and encouraged by what you are doing.

Challenge Four – Facing the Disappointment of Change

It's just plain hard. It's hard to build a business, and it's hard to teach yourself new skills. It's hard to sign-up for things and it's really hard to cold call prospects. It's hard to be received well but then nothing comes of the long phone chats and proposals. Your heart is breaking a little to think that it would have been so much easier not to be moved to make change. How much easier would it be to just be content with Tuesday drinks and a charcuterie board with other retirees? You ask yourself, why am I wired this way? Why am I ambitious and curious about the world and invested in a higher meaning for myself? I'm giving you permission to want more, and if working again or continuing working is what you desire, you need to heed the call. Staying engaged in some manner, humbling yourself and opening your mind to your potential in this life phase can be so freeing. Experiencing the discomfort of letting go of former habits and beliefs means you can stare into the face of uncertainty with confidence and see the best version of yourself. I remember walking into a store, and when I cashed out, I looked up to see my neighbor at the register! I remember him clearly saying: "I just want to work!" Complete and honest clarity! A beautiful message for me and validation that the exquisitely bored are out there doing great things and finding their fulfillment.

Challenge Five – Finding Focus

Have your head down. Focus on what you need right away to get started. Quicker is better. It doesn't have to be perfect but it needs to be something. A phone call, a coffee meeting, a LinkedIn message, something that demonstrates effort and positive action. Once you hit your stride, you will find your comfort level. Your first client, your first interview, your first volunteer session, your first charity event, whatever you align yourself with, finding your focus and concentrating on the big picture is when the magic happens. It means you have established the process, and you feel some level of competence with your way forward. Continue networking and tapping into the things that are driving you; finding depth with your performance is going to bring satisfaction and personal meaning.

Challenge Six – Water off a Duck's Back

Keep going no matter what. For every negative setback there will be a positive opportunity. The energy of your leaning into the tension will serve you well. But don't let the naysayers hold you back. You have clear intentions and your own fulfillment far outweighs anything anyone can say or do to stop your quest. If you are feeling fulfilled and finding meaning, then that's all that matters. There will be slow times and times when things seem to happen all at once. I found it difficult to settle into the cadence of the workload I could handle. Relaxing into the process is part of letting it all unfold.

Challenge Seven – Who Cares

No one cares. No one actually cares what you are working on. It's personal and people are fairly wrapped up in their own daily definition of gratification. You are looking for the new connections that serve, the energy, growth and fulfillment that will be derived from your own initiatives and projects. It's hard when people don't share in your growth, but there are enough who will. You will be more of an example for people than you realize. Leading by doing is infectious and people love a good story! Look for the signs along the way because you are an inspiration, and even though it seems like no one's watching, they most certainly are.

Be kind to yourself in The Shift. It's not an easy phase to experience. It consists of a lot of discomfort and staying grounded is key. Small steps are a solid strategy so you can adjust to what you are seeking. Have an open mind for the growth that you will go through. Learn to accept and own the uncomfortable tensions and the unnerving feelings of putting yourself out there. Your insecurities around learning new skills and expanding your comfort level will be temporary. Companies want to retain experienced workers—we have a more accepting and educated generational population, and the timing is ideal to think of retirement as a new term or entry to your what's next. According to Statistics Canada, among people who have not completely retired but are planning to retire, more than half, 55.1%, report they would continue working if part-time work was an option. We have an engaged work force and an ambitious current and future generation. We also have an up-and-coming generation who have grown up in the work from anywhere in the world mindset. Fractional work is becoming the norm as well. The Shift on a personal level is going to be-

come the accepted norm. We can change our perceptions around age and the professions and roles that
have long been associated with an aging population.

Put The Work In

In The Shift phase, we also have to be willing to put
the work in to stay current, stay relevant and stay
interesting. It's important to not give in to societal
and systemic structures that pigeonhole us into a
segregated and separated demographic. That's on us,
to find innovative and creative ways to stay engaged
with mainstream culture and to find ways of interacting cross generationally. It's not easy because we are
not set up in a social format conducive to exploring
the world so seamlessly in retirement. Embracing
change in The Shift phase and becoming comfortable
with the difficulty it can present is how we can maintain a youthful outlook and keep our cognitive abilities strong. As uncomfortable as it can be, The Shift
is a phase we can look back on and can be grateful
for. Once you land on your *what's next*, you will experience the shift that comes with knowing others are
trusting you and are seeing your value. This is understanding your self-importance and trading your services for value. It will further reinforce the reward you
see from putting the work in.

Patterns of Consistency

The Shift phase leads to consistency. And you're going to need it in the next phase where the hustle happens. The Hustle is where you start building. It's where your actions lie and your plan begins to take place. During The Shift, practice repetition, even if it's having a dedicated work space and spending time in that space on a regular daily basis. Consistency builds momentum which is needed for action. Consistency also starts creating accountability for yourself. Your discipline, habits and routines start to show up. These are areas you will welcome, and the formula always wins. Consistency is the game changer as it grows intent and progress. Whether we are applying for a job or creating our own, consistency loops back to all the attributes we need for creating change.

Since part of The Shift phase deals with others and setting boundaries, developing consistent habits will help us establish more of a routine and maintaining boundaries becomes easier. I think others start to understand that your routine and habits and consistency can build healthy boundaries as you head into other phases where your time will become more focused on specifics. Don't forget that others are sensing The Shift; they are connected to your energy and curious about your efforts. Consistency sets us up for managing the expectations of others while maintaining our own goal alignment. In The Hustle phase we will need consistency to act on what's next. It's an important and crucial way of working that serves us well as we start to really put ourselves out there.

Key Takeaways:

The Shift is not meant to be easy. One may experience discomfort, tension and even fear. But in those moments personal growth is taking place.

Embracing the tension and challenge of The Shift phase often leads to empowerment and empowerment results in action. Become comfortable with the uncomfortable.

Not everyone will agree with or understand your thinking. In this stage, protect your energy and move inward towards contemplation and self-reflection.

Reflections:

Are there people and or activities you could consider taking a break from to set boundaries until you find better alignment?

Can you explore ways to embrace the discomfort in this phase? Can you have faith that it is only temporary? Can you trust the process?

Is there someone that would make a good mentor for what you are needing at this stage directionally?

Finding Your Exquisitely Bored: Actions

1. Find a dedicated work space so that you can start associating the work space with your intentions. This could be a dining room table, a desk, a room corner, somewhere that is strictly your own.

2. Try writing about the things that are making you the most uncomfortable. Is it a lack of a daily routine? Is it lack of interaction with peers? Does it feel like you are losing touch with some of your skills and talent?

3. Try relating the things you wrote down to your new ideas, cross referencing to explore if your new ideas could fulfill some of the missing feelings for you.

EXQUISITELY BORED BLESSINGS

"When we shift our perception, our experience changes." – Lindsay Wagner

....

"The ground beneath you is shifting, and either you get sucked in by holding on to old ways, or you take a giant step forward by taking some risks and seeing what happens." – Bonnie Hammer

....

"Change before you have to." Jack Welsh

....

"To be human is the most ridiculous and most painful and most beautiful incarnation in town. You never know what's coming. It's terrifying, but I'll take it. I'll take the whole ride." – Elizabeth Gilbert

....

"Sail away from the safe harbour. Catch the trade winds in your sails. Explore. Dream. Discover."
– Mark Twain

....

"My destiny is louder than my comfort."
– Yrsa Daley–Ward

....

"I don't know what lies around the bend, but I'm going to believe that the best does." – L. M. Montgomery

....

"Oh my life is changing every day/In every possible way/And oh my dreams/It's never quite as it seems."
– The Cranberries

....

"Anything new we do, creates an opportunity to re-veal parts of ourselves that were hidden." – Paul Jun

....

"When a shift as big as this is imposed on your life, you have no choice but to endure, learn, and reflect."
– Unknown

....

"What do you want? The pain of staying where you are, or the pain of growth?" – J. H. Lasater

....

"Fly on fearful one the world is full of beauty wherev-er you may find it." – Thandi Sliepen

....

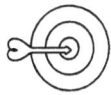

CHAPTER 11
PHASE 6: THE HUSTLE

"You are your own product and service. Build a personal brand that people want and need."
– Exquisitely Bored

Here's where the hustle and the grind happens in order to pull your plan together. I always say that *God is in the details.* Formulate larger goals and under those have clear smaller steps you can achieve on a daily and weekly basis. The tension you have been leaning into is still a part of the process. It's all uncomfortable, and the more you accept the fear just as much as the excitement, the more comfortable you will become with the process. Do you remember The Awakening phase? Was the fear and discomfort not more in that stage? What about The Shift phase? Was it not scary to realize you were not content? That you were meant for something else, something more profound than what you were living? I remember the fear of not making a change being far greater than anything I've encountered in the process thereafter. The more action you take, the less the fear will govern each phase you move through. If you learn to embrace it, you can wire your brain to accept it as part of the change. For every action though, you build further fulfillment towards validating the change. Don't forget: Your principles are attached to your passion and actions. Your actions will lead you to the right people, and your belief in yourself and your emerging plan will be fueled.

Building a Personal Brand

Even if you aren't starting your own business, your new personal brand can help communicate your intent. Find a catchy name and a phrase you can use as a tagline that clearly articulates what you do. Even if you aren't building a business, having an image and mantra for your personal brand can help. You are transforming, and having a picture of how you see yourself is paramount to acting in alignment with your directive. Social media platforms are an ideal way to communicate your personal and/or business brand and build a presence that also keeps you current and relevant. If you don't know how to use social media, learn. These platforms are built in user-friendly ways, and frankly, there is no excuse not to be on social media. Social media is how we maintain connections in a modern-day world. You can curate your news feed to inform your interests, stay connected to family and friends, and form new connections. It's also how networking happens, and not all networking needs to be in person. Social applications offer many avenues to meet and learn from experts, leaders and others in the same life phase as yourself.

You are your own product or service. Being known for something is the hook you need to build a distinct personal brand. Personal branding is the art of building a persona, a story and a perception about your own self for others to have a better understanding of you as a whole person. It's a way to guide the narrative about yourself in a positive way and to maintain control of the information you say about yourself. The exercise of building a personal brand is also a way to reveal the attributes and characteristics tied to your passions and talents that can attract others to you. When you start communicating a clear definition of self, you will develop further clarity and intent. In previous chapters when I talk about the three Ps: principles, passion and people, nowhere else is there a better place to communicate these than through personal branding. Values and beliefs are a key foundation to your brand, and attaching your content to these is a way to demonstrate and live out your brand in action. If you decide to start a business or take another job, matching your business persona to your personal brand is a good idea as well. This helps to reinforce your story and continues to communicate and market your value as a person and an employee. If you are taking courses or enrolled in continuing education, social media is the way to connect with others building skills in the same field. This helps build a personal support network and leads to expanding your network. It's also a part of your personal brand story and builds interest around you as a person and your personality.

Building And Believing In Your Personal Value

Personal values are your own beliefs and principles. They guide and direct your real-world experience, time investment and interests. Often, upon retiring, people become disillusioned and confused about personal values and how to use those to build meaning and satisfaction in their next term. In The Awakening phase, I noticed my alignment with my personal values happening. The things I valued and put importance on were where I wanted to put my focus. Because I'm passionate about my values, I was able to directly connect them to what my exquisitely bored would be. I also think the word "value" and "values" differ slightly. Values are what I've defined above and tend to be actual tangible beliefs, ideals and principles. Likely things that have been part of our emotional DNA from how we were raised and socialized. When we look at the singular as "value," I see this as a

form of self-worth. In retirement, since we've discon-
nected from our world as we once knew it, and often
because we are aging, our inclination to attribute value to our personal brand and our skills can diminish.
Because of the segregation in society that happens
to retirees, we aren't necessarily connecting to people and places that help us express or demonstrate
our value. I connect our value to being paid for our
skills, services and products that we create, curate
and serve up to the world. When you reframe the
confidence that comes with moving through these
phases, you begin to see transactional value for yourself, and that in turn increases our belief in ourselves
and what we have to offer. Value and values need to
match our behaviours. If you want to be paid for your
skills you need to take actionable steps toward finding payment. If your value set is guiding you to your
passion, then you need to take action to work toward
something that involves the thing or things you are
passionate about. Values are not just static, invisible
things. They are actionable directives that guide and
lead us to where we belong in order to realize fulfillment and a meaningful life.

Define What You Need

Do you need sales? Do you need a product? Do you
need a website? An updated resume? Figure out the

tools you need to succeed. Maybe you don't need an entire website, maybe just a page. Then find the people in your network who can help. Ask questions, meet for coffee, consult with your mentor and be purposeful in how you start to build your tool kit. Don't overcomplicate this part. Start small but at least start. Sometimes it's been a long while since we have had to do a resume or update our work profile. Look for other examples online, notice the patterns and start extrapolating your own key selling features and call attention to those. Find others who are motivating and inspirational to be around. Attend events, and see what you gravitate to as it's highly likely that's where you will find your people.

Market Yourself

Again, you may not be selling a product or offering a direct service. Perhaps you are taking a course, contributing to a charity, finding a higher purpose of some sort. Wherever your fulfillment takes you, market yourself accordingly. Think of how powerful your personal network is. How can you use your network to build depth for your exquisitely bored? People want to help more than it feels like they do. Having a personal brand acts as your cover story and marketing yourself involves being out there. Be in as many places as you can, hand cards out, talk with intent.

It's okay to explain you are exploring opportunities if you haven't quite defined your plan yet. You will be surprised at the inspiration that arises from where you least expect it. This happened to me, and chances are you are doing these things alone. I felt great self-awareness in this stage and being alone at events allowed me to experience the people around me fully and completely.

Attending events alone allows for deeper focus. Marketing yourself is all about increasing your visibility. People need to learn if you are available for work, or if you have a product or service to offer. This is a great stage to test your market needs. What are people's reactions when you explain your ideas and intentions? What are the kinds of questions they are asking? I also found that explaining my business over and over again allowed me to develop a concise and rehearsed version of it. Over time I could explain it with clarity, and depending on my audience I was able to finesse my elevator pitch for an even further refined message. Sometimes it's clear in our own minds, but putting it to words can be difficult. Using events and networking was essential for me to understand how Exquisitely Bored as a company was landing on people in general. This was the most valuable stage for feedback for me and I was encouraged by the groundswell of people's energy and interest in what I was building.

Find Your Peers

Remember those peers you left behind with the retirement cake, dirty plates and forks? Perhaps they can be of use in your network along with the many new peers you will meet as you tap into the new. The more you focus on your passions, the more relevant connections you will make. Your new peers will directly correlate to your intentions. There will be an energy and momentum you gain from discovering these new connections.

Find Your Fans

Social media is a powerful marketing tool. Use your channels to explain your business and set your intent. Your fans aren't just online; they can be anyone aspirational who believes in your mandate. The closer you become to exactly what you are envisioning, the more fans, as supporters, will emerge. Talking about your plan to anyone who will listen can produce new connections and open doors. The ebb and flow of socializing your skills and desires is part of an ongoing process. You may as well become comfortable with the self-advocacy that you will need to do in The Hustle phase.

Track Your Path

Once you write something down it becomes more real. A thought put to pen and paper becomes an action. Keeping a list of three or four things you need to do each day to work toward your path will build accountability and progress over time. Treat your tracking list like a job. Own it like you would an actual project. Show up for it each day and check off completed tasks. Your brain will begin to believe the logic that the list creates. Your intentions become actual projects instead of just emotions and wants. You don't lose weight just thinking about it; you attach actions to changing habits and track your dietary intake. This translates to something real for your brain that can start building the belief and evidence that what you are accomplishing is real.

If you can see the tasks completed and checked off visually, you can start to believe that you are making the change. The proof is in hand, and your brain cannot dispute that accomplishments have taken place. Staying single focused is a tactic that I found made me concentrate on just one win at a time. First it was a logo and that was all I focused on until it felt right. Then I moved to a business card format and focused intently on creating something tangible and real where I could see my brand and my intent come to life. Can you relate to checking things off a list? The psychology of list checking is a very real thing and directly correlates to goal setting and completion.

Once you find the events and opportunities connected to your interests and passions, participate and observe. What is resonating? Is it an opportunity to work in a setting surrounded by products and services you love? Is it an opportunity to just be with other people and interact? Is it an opportunity for income? Financial goals can be the driver just as much as any other intention. Money comes when we feel connected to the value that we are trading our time and skills for.

True change won't come without putting the work in. It requires consistent action toward a plan. If you need to change your environment, then do so. Find an area to work in that becomes your own personal space. Having a zone that connects you to your purpose allows you to separate your efforts from the noise and distractions of daily life. More than anything, be flexible. Your ideas can evolve, and once you get started, it will become increasingly clear where you need to be.

Key Takeaways:

Start building your personal brand. You can also attach your business persona to your personal brand.

Take actionable steps towards understanding your value and how you can generate income from your pursuit.

Define what you need and start marketing yourself. Use tools like social media and connections to communicate your value proposition and take consistent action towards your plan.

Reflections:

What is resonating most for you? Is it an opportunity to work in a setting surrounded by products and services you love?

Is it an opportunity to be with other people and interact?

Is it an opportunity for income? Financial goals can be the driver just as much as any other intention. Money comes when we feel connected to the value that we are trading our time and skills for.

Finding Your Exquisitely Bored: Actions

1. If your vision is to embark on something on your own terms, design your business card and create a tagline for your business.

2. Track the three or four things you need to accomplish each day.

3. Commit to your social media channels and each day update your content to begin marketing yourself.

EXQUISITELY BORED BLESSINGS

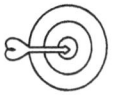

"Peace of mind produces right values, right values produce right thoughts. Right thoughts produce right actions" – Mark Richardson

"Values are like fingerprints. Nobody has the same but you leave them all over everything you do."
– Elvis Presley

"Keep your thoughts positive because your thoughts become your words. Keep your words positive because your words become your behaviour. Keep your behaviour positive because your behaviour becomes your habits. Keep your habits positive because your habits become your values. Keep your values positive because your values become your destiny"
– Mahatma Gandhi

"A highly–developed values system is like a compass. It serves as a guide to point you in the right direction when you are lost." – Idowu Koyenikan

"Effectiveness without values is a tool without a purpose." – Edward de Bono

....

"Happiness is that state of consciousness which proceeds from the achievement of one's values."
– Ayn Rand

....

"Anything that changes your values changes your behaviour." – George Sheehan

....

"Lasting change is a series of compromises. And compromise is all right, as long your values don't change."
– Jane Goodall

....

"It's not hard to make decisions when you know what your values are." – Roy Disney

....

"The difference between a successful person and others is not a lack of strength, not a lack of knowledge, but rather a lack of will." – Vince Lombardi

....

"The important thing is not to stop questioning. Curiosity has its own reason for existing. One cannot help but be in awe when he contemplates the mysteries of eternity, of life, of the marvelous structure of reality. It is enough if one tries merely to comprehend a little of this mystery every day. Never lose a holy curiosity."
– Albert Einstein

....

CHAPTER 12
PHASE 7: BACK TO THE GRIND

"Work, is that you knocking? Come in my friend, we've only just begun."
– Exquisitely Bored

In this case, going back to the grind is not a bad thing! It means you have found direction and clarity around what you will be working at! Perhaps you have decided to start your own business or work part time somewhere. Whatever it is, you welcome the grind and are ready for a more meaningful and fulfilling lifestyle. You are officially part of the exquisitely bored club! We are living life on our own terms; we are ambitious, driven and eager to make our next mark. When I started my business, I was most driven by finding fulfillment and delving into something I was passionate about. I engineered Exquisitely Bored from a place of principles and passion. I didn't have all the talent I needed, so I taught myself what was missing and a few mentors guided me through getting started. Then the money followed. Passion is not enough on its own to guarantee the financial. But it does fuel perseverance and an acute gut feeling about where to take your focus. You also have to structure a business with a clear plan and financial strategy.

Work That Rolodex

After decades in the workforce, use your own network to tap into mentors and find advice to create your business plan. Understanding what to charge for services, how to structure your business, accounting best practices, trademarking and other details are part of the plan you will need to build. Passion alone can't build and sustain a business. But what if you were to find a category you are passionate about and attach that to problem solving for others or filling a gap? What if you applied to work in a role completely different from your career but it got you up in the morning, gave you a routine and provided a sense of fulfillment? You would have peers, a sense of accomplishment throughout the work day and compensation for your contribution.

Volunteering

Attaching yourself to something that holds meaning for you on a deep personal level can even involve volunteering. I'm not sure everyone understands the importance of cognitive function. Even volunteering presents an opportunity to learn new skills, and the benefit that community engagement has on our well-being is massively taken for granted. Feeling like we belong to our community and that we contribute something greater than ourselves is part of building the legacy that can live on after us. We know that self-esteem takes a hit in retirement, and as we age, if we make efforts to boost our sense of our place in the world and build further on our already diverse work backgrounds, we can feed our confidence, make a difference and affect positive outcomes. Social networks attached to volunteering are full of potential. If you base your volunteering on your principles and passions, you will find others with similar strengths, beliefs and interests.

Your Encore

What if we were to reframe retirement and use words like *"term"* instead? Are you starting a new *"work term?"* Seeing retirement as simply another phase would remove stigma, labelling and things like ageism. We barely talk about the state of healthy living that working on into retirement has been proven to offer. Research from Merrill Lynch indicates that "nearly a quarter of today's retirees do some work for pay, but a whopping 73% of pre-retirees expect to work after they officially retire – up from 68% who said the same in 2022." I think the research is also indicating that not a lot of people can actually afford to retire. Whether we come to this conclusion by being forced or through our own financial free will, it's time to turn the narrative upside down.

The Obituary Factor

This is something I've coined to provoke reflection and introspection. Imagine if someone were to read your obituary, what would it be? Having a place in a retirement community has allowed me the privilege to read many obituaries. I've noticed the ones that stand out. They list the meaningful work, the organizational contributions and the dedication to something beyond their own personal gain. How do you want your obituary to be read? With this frame, I think we can get my point that our skills and our abilities are far beyond what we perceive ourselves to be capable of during this term in our lives. Our mortality sits before us in retirement like a looming unknown. We may have decades before our number comes up and yet we acquiesce to this systemic place that we are relegated to. Getting back to the grind is an opportunity for a host of benefits, benefits that allow us not only to find meaning for ourselves but also affect others with our meaningful work. Whether it's giving back, finding a sense of purpose or feeling rewarded, there are non-monetary upsides to finding our *what's next.*

Key Takeaways:

You have found your focus and are starting to take consistent actions.

Use your network to tap into connections that can use your services and products.

Attach to something that holds meaning for you. Volunteering can build confidence and expand our social networks. Whether it's giving back, finding a sense of purpose or feeling rewarded, there are non-monetary upsides to finding our *what's next.*

Reflections:

How would you want your obituary to read? What notable things would you want people to read and discover about you?

How can we start turning the retirement narrative upside down?

What if we were to lose the term "retirement" entirely and instead focus on it as a "work term?"

Finding Your Exquisitely Bored: Actions

1. Identify what problem you are solving for your audience. Make a clear mission statement for how you are filling a gap with your role or your efforts.

2. Work with your mentor or network to clarify your pricing strategy and be sure to secure your sense of value you are receiving for your skills and talent.

3. Research ways you can become an authority and a credible resource for what you have identified as your niche. Write a blog post or create a social media post to reinforce your personal and business brand to your followers.

EXQUISITELY BORED BLESSINGS

"The only way to do great work is to love what you do. If you haven't found it yet, keep looking. Don't settle. As with all matters of the heart, you'll know when you find it." – Steve Jobs

....

"Success is not the key to happiness. Happiness is the key to success. If you love what you are doing, you will be successful." – Albert Schweitzer

....

"You don't have to be great to start, but you have to start to be great." – Zig Ziglar

....

"The difference between try and triumph is just a little umph!" – Marvin Phillips

....

"There are no shortcuts to any place worth going."
– Beverly Sills

....

"The successful warrior is the average man, with laser-like focus." – Bruce Lee

....

"Don't let yesterday take up too much of today."
– Will Rogers

"I have not failed. I've just found 10,000 ways that won't work." – Thomas A. Edison

"The only limit to our realization of tomorrow will be our doubts of today." – Franklin D. Roosevelt

"The harder I work, the luckier I get."
– Samuel Goldwyn

"I attribute my success to this: I never gave or took any excuse." – Florence Nightingale

"A dream doesn't become reality through magic; it takes sweat, determination, and hard work."
– Colin Powell

"Success is not how high you have climbed, but how you make a positive difference to the world."
– Roy T. Bennett

"Opportunities are usually disguised as hard work, so most people don't recognize them." – Ann Landers

CHAPTER 13
PHASE 8: THE LAW OF ATTRACTION

"Motion and action create energy, energy for finding your principles, passion and people."
– Exquisitely Bored

I absolutely believe in this philosophy. This has played out like a textbook in my quest to understand my exquisitely bored mindset and to expand on what that could be for my future. As soon as I started to picture the kind of clients I wanted to work with and the type of content I wanted to create, those people and things literally showed up at my doorstep. Science cannot prove this law, but if it helps a person with their mindset and approach, then what harm is there in believing?

In retirement I believe we are even more set up to succeed. It's a unique circumstance in that we have already had an accomplished career, mastered a skill set and spent time in the trenches. Our confidence can come from the fact that we already have a resume of varied roles and a tenure along with the positive and negative outcomes of our work experience.

Reaching the state of being exquisitely bored is one of the most beautiful places you can be in your mature work life. It is a state of living life on your own terms, vibrating at your highest level of talent and passion and in turn using your background of career experience and skill set to bring fulfillment and value to a new way of working. Those who recognize the exquisitely bored potential are the benefactors of work outputs and team players that improve productivity, speed to market and ultimately results that only those with experienced tenure can offer.

For the exquisitely bored, it is a time to be discovered and realized, as your skills, passion and desire to continue adding value to the work world can be accessed by employers requiring experienced and exceptional talent for their businesses. Or as part of building a foundation for your own business. I call it: retiring to success.

When you start your networking, you will be amazed at the connections you start to attract. Your reaching out will be met with curiosity and openness for the most part from others. People appreciate hard work and effort. When others see your efforts and hear your story, they are only too willing to help.

Each new connection is buoyed by a sense of learning, understanding and realizing the human condition. There is an attraction for others in your being vulnerable. In putting yourself out there for business or for relationship building. A connection is a way of experiencing a positive emotion. And I believe that whether it's spirituality or mindset, whatever your own personal philosophy, you will attract the right person at the right time for what you require next. If it's not the person directly, then it's a one-degree connection that can unfold as something useful for your business or idea. It's not magic; it's simply a "can do" mindset. I also think your state of mind is key for attracting what you need. Coming from a place of passion and "I want this" is inspiring for others connecting with you.

Where and what we focus our attention on is key. We'll likely be talking to and meeting others who share our interests and passions. When they see and feel this reciprocated, half the work is done. They see an easy and effortless way to accept help and service from someone. And if it's a business you are building, this could be your first customer or client! You have shifted your identity from retired person to employed person or owner, founder, creator, whatever your pursuit is. By this stage, you have done the prep work, and you identify so much with your new pursuit that you are living it. It's like a while back when I described the to-do list of working toward your goals as being already like your business. The to-do list becomes your new work. You start acting like you are already working. Your energy has to match the new life you want to create. It's like role playing. If you mimic what you want and how you see it unfolding, you will be ready to receive it.

Having your brand and brand identity in the form of a logo is a big part of already seeing yourself open for business. You've done the self-reflection a few phases ago, and now it's about attracting the people you need in order to make your business or goals a reality. Whatever you are giving your attention and focus to will be what emerges in your path. You are likely driven at this stage to be living and breathing everything that can move you forward. Your old context did not serve you. As a result, the extreme focus at this stage is going to reward you with abundance. If your product or service can in turn help someone else you are connecting with fulfill their goals, you have filled a gap for their betterment and can establish a need for you to be part of their equation. Your personal growth mindset is part of the chain of events but so is your action. Every meeting you book, every interaction you organize, will build further on your unwavering desire for change.

Surrounding yourself with similar energy at this stage is imperative to attracting the right outcomes. Sometimes putting on hold certain interactions with friends may serve you well in the long run. If the energy and results you seek are not matched with your current interactions, it will be difficult to see results. You have to also have done the work in The Awareness and The Shift phase because putting the work in is the way forward. Behaviour, discipline and motion are the sustained efforts required to find your way. Your goals are tied to your principles, and research shows that when values and beliefs are tied to our principles, we have an increased chance of accomplishing passion-fueled goals instead of materialistic ones. In retirement we are more likely to be fueled by change that fulfills and provides meaning. This is why the exquisitely bored are perfectly poised to attract abundance. We are truly looking to fulfill gaps that are formulated from deep within. Our life learning has provided us with the awareness to know the difference. Sure, the money will follow, but our ambitions and our need for fulfillment are wider than our wallets in that we desire to stay relevant, interested and engaged in the world around us. These are the powerful forces driving us.

Do not take the law of attraction for granted—it's moving the right people into your path and you are sending signals to others in the same mindset. Do the work in the previous phases and be ready to receive!

Key Takeaways:

You will start to attract other curious and notable connections. You will be "retiring to success," as your network starts to expand to receive you as well as putting new people in your path.

Surround yourself with similar energy to ensure you attract the right outcomes.

We have an increased chance of accomplishing passion-fueled goals instead of materialistic ones. In retirement we are more likely to be fueled by change that fulfills and provides meaning.

Reflections:

Are you surprised by the kind of people attracted to your cause? Are you meeting interesting and helpful connections for your efforts?

Reflect on the quality of connections that have crossed your path. Can you feel the encouragement? Do you start to believe more in the power of an open mind and a curious spirit?

Are you seeing that where you put your energy and focus tends to be where you see the most traction?

Finding Your Exquisitely Bored: Actions

1. Identify three exceptional contacts that feel out of your league to make contact with.

2. Ask someone you are now working with to put you in contact with someone they feel would be a prospect for you.

3. Do one or two things extra for a client or in your role that reinforces your feeling of fulfillment beyond just the monetary.

EXQUISITELY BORED BLESSINGS

"See the things that you want as already yours. Know that they will come to you at need. Then let them come. Don't fret and worry about them. Don't think about your lack of them. Think of them as yours, as belonging to you, as already in your possession."
– Robert Collier

....

"Nothing is, unless our thinking makes it so."
– Shakespeare

....

"I attract to my life whatever I give my attention, energy and focus to, whether positive or negative."
– Michael Losier

....

"That which is like unto itself is drawn."
– Jerry and Esther Hicks

....

"Whatever you create in your life you must first create in your imagination." – Tycho Photiou

....

"Cherish your visions and your dreams as they are the children of your soul, the blueprints of your ultimate achievements." – Napoleon Hill

....

"A man is but the product of his thoughts. What he thinks he becomes." – Gandhi

....

"Everyone visualizes whether he knows it or not. Visualizing is the great secret of success."
– Genevieve Berhrend

....

"What you think you become. What you feel you attract. What you imagine you create." – Buddha

....

"Whether you think you can or think you can't, either way you are right." – Henry Ford

....

"You create your thoughts, your thoughts create your intentions and your intentions create your reality."
– Wayne Dyer

....

"When you are inspired by some great purpose, some extraordinary project, all your thoughts break their bonds." – Patanjali

....

"Thoughts become things. If you see it in your mind, you will hold it in your hand." – Bob Procto

....

"Whatever you hold in your mind on a consistent basis is exactly what you will experience in your life."
– Tony Robbins

....

"You are deserving of whatever you want. You truly are. This is one of the most important truths you can come to understand." – Bob Doyle

....

CHAPTER 14
PHASE 9: EVOLUTION AND GROWTH

"Fixed thinking is for the safe players and guarantees a fixed income."
– Exquisitely Bored

At this stage you have put your shingle out into the universe and are actively engaged in growing your business, building your network and understanding exactly what it is you are doing. This could also take the form of volunteering, aligning with a charity, finding a hobby or spending time with family. It's about finding your fulfillment and building a life that continues to be filled with meaning, ambition and relevance. You have found the thing that gives you contentment, a sense of pride, satisfaction and a peaceful feeling. The premise here is to tap into the lasting state that comes with a sense of well-being. It's a calmness that radiates and carries you through even difficult times, as those will present as life sees fit.

This personal growth phase is very connected to the

efforts and actions directed toward your business or wherever you've landed as your source of fulfillment. I found this to be one of the easier phases because you are simply building on what you have started. The further you go into the detail and specific goals you have set, the more you and your creation grow and evolve. Your business may evolve into more than you thought possible, or you may streamline efforts or switch up your focus entirely. The beauty of this phase is that things are working themselves out to align with your actions. My exquisitely bored evolved from something specific into a broader range of skill sets, some of which I wasn't entirely confident with, but I was able to grow into my abilities and believe in myself.

Personal growth is simply self-development. It may consist of learning a new skill to help your progress along or changing a behaviour. I cannot stress the importance of continuous learning enough. Building on what you already know, as well as developing new knowledge, is the process of life-long learning. The world around you is in constant flux, and retirement is a sure buzzkill for staying relevant and interesting. Build a desire and drive to stay curious and intrigued by expanding your world. Travel is great, but it's regular. Everyone else is doing it, and going to the same places that travel trends dictate is not going to make you as inter-esting as you potentially can be. Become one with your neuroplasticity! Our brain is able to adapt and reorganize throughout our life if we feed it. We can actually form new synapses based on new infor-mation, experiences and challenges. In the preser-vation phase, our brain requires sharpening, and mitigating cognitive decline helps formulate new connections and increased brain function. Chal-lenging yourself with new skills and uncomfortable interactions and stretching your abilities will all add to your sense of fulfillment, confidence and well-being. If we are already battling age and the limitations that society imposes on us because of a number, it's dangerous to think of coming across "old" when there are efforts we can make to main-tain our youthful energy and disposition.

Perception is reality. The way we perceive retirement is entirely different from its reality. Many of us are prepared when it comes to financial needs, but it's the non-financial needs that trip us up. There are many institutions more than willing to help us reach our financial goals, but as far as social needs, emo-tional needs, personal desires and such, the various aspects of a retirement far exceed just the financial. The Defined Contribution Institutional Investment Association records that 83% of retirees returned to work by choice, not out of necessity. For such an important stage of life, you would think we would spend more time preparing and assessing people outside of finance. Near retirees have an inordinate amount of stress around what retirement looks like financially, and I think a great deal of this anxiety could be lessened by the knowledge that 83% are returning to work and it's preferable to prepare to have an extended phase of your life that can not only support you financially but emotionally. I think taking the pressure off this being a 65 or die decision transforms it into a segue to a new phase of life. Forward looking planning needs to encompass how we can meet our emotional and social needs along with financial ones. It's about creating a picture of the life you desire in retirement. We need to emotionally connect retirees to what they want out of their retired life, their families, their emotional needs and other such informed decisions.

Part of growth is accepting who and what you are after work. A loss of identity is normal along with social consistency. Many of us related to who we were at work and what we chose as a career path. Our identity was tied up in the type of work we did and our skill set. How do we define the new us and then grow from there? It's about building an entirely new lifestyle, and the transition is daunting.

The growth mindset sees you growing and improving in your abilities. A fixed mindset sees you taking the easy route and viewing your talents and skill set as fixed. I feel like the kind of schooling we grew up with was more of a fixed mindset approach. It educated us with the masses, whereas in retirement we have the privilege of exploring a more individual growth mindset. The same triggers that would have inhibited our growth mindset in the workplace, hopefully, are no longer the same barriers. Triggers like comparing ourselves to others, working in a competitive environment and facing criticism are not as paramount.

The challenge in retirement is thought patterns that emerge telling us we are too old, too tired, too irrelevant. There is never a lack of things to send us off in the wrong direction. Attached to this is the question of "Who do you spend the most time around?" You know the old adage of becoming like the top five people you spend your time around. I think there is a great deal of substance to this when it comes to retirement and a growth mindset. There are those who are content and fulfilled in many different ways. Those ways may not be your ways. Perhaps their ways and habits encompass limited thinking and are filled with fears. They are the safe players. When you look at your circle and what serves you for what's next, refusing to settle and surrounding yourself with those who take action will be a powerful force in moving you forward to the kind of fulfillment you deserve. Choose your circle selectively and raise the bar to match where you want to go. The people around us will shape our direction and actions.

Key Takeaways:

Personal growth is connected to the actions and efforts that you are undertaking. Your source of fulfillment has emerged and you can identify the direction you need to move towards.

We need to connect retirees to their emotional needs around what they want to get out of their new phase. It's not just about the financial piece; it's as much about the emotional and social requirements and defining the new you.

A growth mindset has moved through the acceptance phase and sees continued learning as an integral part of the process. It does not subscribe to fixed thinking.

Reflections:

If retirement allows us to pursue a more individual growth mindset, what are things for you personally that have emerged as key learnings?

Since the people around us shape our direction and actions, do you feel you have the right people around you to meet your goals?

Do you feel your age? What perception do you think people have of your age?

Finding Your Exquisitely Bored: Actions

1. Write down the top five people you spend the most time with. Do these align with where you feel you are headed as it pertains to finding meaning in your life?

2. List a few people you have recently come into contact with who are examples of how and what you want to be.

3. Make a note of a new skill that you would like to develop to add to your goal set.

EXQUISITELY BORED BLESSINGS

"Be not afraid of growing slowly; be afraid only of standing still." – Chinese Proverb

"True life is lived when tiny changes occur."
– Leo Tolstoy

"Life isn't about finding yourself. Life is about creating yourself." – Bernard Shaw

"Change and growth take place when a person has risked himself and dares to become involved with experimenting with his own life." – Herbert Otto

"The fact is, that to do anything in the world worth doing, we must not stand back shivering and thinking of the cold and danger but jump in and scramble as well as we can." – Robert Cushing

"The highest reward for one's toil is not what one gets for it, but what one becomes by it." – John Ruskin

"Motivation is what gets you started. Habit is what keeps you going." – Jim Ryun

....

"Great works are performed not by strength but by perseverance." – Samuel Johnson

....

"Life belongs to the living, and he who lives must be prepared for changes."
– Johann Wolfgang von Goethe

....

"Words are where most change begins."
– Brandon Sanderson

....

"True life is lived when tiny changes occur."
– Leo Tolstoy

....

"To improve is to change; to be perfect is to change often." – Winston S. Churchill

....

"Act as if what you do makes a difference. It does."
– William James

....

"Change the way you look at things and the things you look at change." – Wayne W. Dyer

....

CHAPTER 15
PHASE 10: THE CONNECTOR MINDSET

"I've never introduced two people whom I couldn't imagine figuring something out for the betterment of themselves or even the world."
– Exquisitely Bored

At this stage you have started thinking differently about your world as you knew it. The connector mindset means you see possibilities and potential where you didn't before. In your excitement about learning, working, volunteering or finding your fulfillment in whatever that may be, your desire and frame of mind are about how we can all work together. The personal growth mindset makes you aspirational in that you want others to succeed. You see opportunities to connect the dots for others. Because you have now put yourself out there, by doing something either in your same work genre or entirely different, you now possess a desire to see others succeed. The gratification you receive from helping someone else becomes a very real part of your own success. When you see someone in the same position as you, you can recognize the power you hold with one simple introduction.

The younger generation are enormously in need of your connector mindset. With your decades of experience and your principled approach, you have a great deal of skill and knowledge to help mobilize an entire future generation. Never take for granted the learning, skill set and ability to guide and mentor that your work life has provided. With each new connection you make for yourself, there are further connections that will emerge for those around you. The "how can we work together" mindset is one of discovery, possibility and what ifs. Connectors are known to make things happen easier and quicker. This is an extremely important frame of mind if you decide to re-enter the workforce or build your own fulfillment. The act of connecting just makes for happier, more content people. You are never too old to be a connector. Connecting begins with conversations.

Connector Conversations

Some of the conversations you will have around connecting people likely won't have anything to do with your business or motives at that moment. It can simply be about spotting an opportunity in which two people need to meet who share common industries, like-minded goals or a product or service that the other person can use. Ultimately, it's the energy and excitement you take from making those connections that can fuel your own motives. Connecting with others presents opportunities to brainstorm, ideate and re-ignite your own creative flow along the way. The confidence that you will find in networking and connecting is enormous. When people react to your own initiative and ideas, you are fueled to continue the momentum and the impact.

Connector conversations also allow you to stay current. When we are open to continuous learning, we begin to understand how important conversations are to build knowledge about the changing world around us. Expertise outside of our own realm and comfort level is imperative to test our self-assurance and ability to work through challenges we may come across. When you expand your thinking to be more about "we" as a group and the universe as a pool of other talents and information sources, you become empowered beyond your own limited thinking. We have to realize that as we age, the tendencies to restrict our thinking and reluctance to learn new things is a research-supported reality. It will naturally become more difficult to see new perspectives and to adopt new ideas. I like to think that we all won't have this tendency to the same extent—there will always be those with an inclination to stay curious and cognitively flexible.

Connections For Growth

The ability to foster connections with not only ourselves but also through connections with others increases our sense of purpose. When we see ourselves facilitating important connections and building relationships, we are more likely to respect differing opinions and perspectives. Having a support system with other entrepreneurs and those in the same life stage can help us build resilience, receive constructive criticism and contribute to our sense of overall well-being. Connections bring growth personally and professionally. We will always get more than we expect when we connect with others. As we age, we typically have less fear about connecting, and in this stage, we need the options for anything and everything connected to our goals and ambitions that can lead towards fulfillment.

Connection as Personal Brand

I found that connecting others to one another helped take me outside of my own head. I felt empowered after making a connection and in turn used that to build further momentum for my business. A connector mindset can directly correlate to your personal brand. The more connections you make, the more you can directly turn the spotlight on to your own brand. This provides you with influence and advantage that can open more doors to help meet your own goals. Becoming a valuable resource for others means you see others as they are; it means you value and respect others and can form an authentic connection. But it's also currency, and this means being remembered when others see an opportunity for you in return. Remember the popular Maya Angelou quote: *"People will forget what you said, people will forget what you did, but people will never forget how you made them feel."* This is the premise of creating healthy, effective experiences through interactions that are often more impressionable than words or actions. Discover and keep the connector attitude, and your personal brand will flourish. Connecting with others leads to the road of your own defined purpose.

Connection as Inspiration

Consider finding other businesses or individuals doing what appeals to you. What about their personas, accomplishments or ideas are what you see for yourself? Using connection as a means to inspiration is an extremely powerful method of meeting your goals quicker. Attending events, researching similar products and services or reading books and accounts of successful examples can be ways of understanding how to build your new identity in retirement. Striving for the same accomplishments and then applying your own values and principles means you can see where someone else's passion and skill set led them. It's not about copying someone else, but rather finding similar strategies that can be applied to accelerate your growth. Your path will be your own unique way, your own style and your own authentic brand. Conceptually, there is a lot of learning in the world around us. Being inspired by others is an important step to finding our own fulfillment and meaningful direction.

Key Takeaways:

When you are seeing success and excitement around your new initiatives, you will want the same for others. Connecting others gives you a sense of joy, and the collaboration allows them to share in your success.

When we facilitate other connections, we are more likely to be open to new perspectives.

Connecting others directly correlates to your own personal brand. It is a reflection of what you are building and who you are becoming personally and professionally.

Reflections:

Do you see a correlation between the people you have connected, and as a result, what attributes do they share?

What skills do you have that the younger generation could benefit from?

What businesses and people are inspiring you, and how can you tap into their strategies and tactics for your own growth?

Finding Your Own Exquisitely Bored: Actions

1. Find an example of a business or person that most replicates what you are trying to create.

2. Spend time on your LinkedIn profile and aim to connect two people in the next month.

3. Write a list of the top people who have supported you consistently throughout your journey.

EXQUISITELY BORED BLESSINGS

"The true value of networking doesn't come from how many people we can meet but rather how many people we can introduce to others." – Simon Sinek

"You can have everything in life you want, if you will just help other people get what they want."
– Zig Ziglar

"Technology is nothing. What's important is that you have faith in people, that they're basically good and smart, and if you give them tools, they'll do wonderful things with them." – Steve Jobs

"Networking that matters is helping people achieve their goals" – Seth Godin

"Networking is not about just connecting people. It's about connecting people with people, people with ideas, and people with opportunities."
– Michele Jennae

"You can close more business in two months by becoming interested in other people than you can in two years by trying to get people interested in you."
– Dale Carnegie

"Ask not what your network can do for you. Ask what you can do for your network." – Greg Bahlmann

"Networking is simply the cultivation of mutually beneficial, give–and–take, win–win relationships. It works best, however, when emphasizing the 'give' part."
– Bob Burg

"In our global, networked economy, you can't allow your social capital to lie dormant. Reinvest."
– Porter Gale

"I define connection as the energy that exists between people when they feel seen, heard, and valued; when they can give and receive without judgement; and when they derive sustenance and strength from the relationship." – Brené Brown

"The whole idea of compassion is based on a keen awareness of the interdependence of all these living beings, which are all part of one another, and all involved in one another." – Thomas Merton

"Eventually everything connects – people, ideas, objects. The quality of the connections is the key to quality per se." – Charles Eames

....

"I am a part of all that I have met." – Lord Tennyson

....

"A thousand fibers connect us with our fellow men. Our actions run as causes, and they come back to us as effects." – Herman Melville

....

"We humans are social beings. We come into the world as the result of others' actions. We survive here in dependence on others. Whether we like it or not, there is hardly a moment of our lives when we do not benefit from others' activities. For this reason, it is hardly surprising that most of our happiness arises in the context of our relationships with others."
–The Dalai Lama

....

CHAPTER 16
PHASE 11: SLOW AND STEADY

"Take your time with the process. It's like hang-ing clothes to dry: eventually they dry but it's hard to wait sometimes."
– Exquisitely Bored

You've hung your shingle. Your principles, passion and people are working together for what feels like a more rewarding lifestyle. We know that slow and steady wins the race. Patience with ourselves to relax into what we've built, the changes we've made and the progress we've realized are important for the lon-gevity of our success.

The natural inclination is to feel like we need to keep building on the momentum. If we've seen accelerated growth and results, we may feel the need to stay in the build phase, and there may have been an inten-sity to our process and thinking over the last while. However, it's important to realize this phase of our life for what it is, fulfillment, meaning and continuous learning. While we are receiving those tenets, it's okay to still have a part of retirement that rewards our decades of hard work. I found it natural to fall back into the hustle; after all, I spent more of my life in that mindset and it's not going to dissipate overnight. There are amazing stories of retiree accomplishments. And if the goal is to succeed beyond measure, then by all means keep the momentum! But even the topmost successful entrepreneurs out there didn't take a wild risk and leap off a cliff. They will all tell you that they followed a slow and steady incremental method while they worked towards their bigger picture. Some even had other jobs while they were building their future state.

This is the part of retirement planning for which I don't understand the lack of exposure. Preparing while we are still working would be helpful for asking the questions about where we want to see ourselves and what we picture doing. Using your employed skills to further build toward what you see yourself doing in retirement and having a clear path forward is missing in many educational facets around retirement literature, planning and advice. While it's true that no one can tell you what's right for you, someone asking questions and helping you define directionally could set you on a path much sooner. This would also remove a lot of stress and the unknown that younger generations are faced with today when it comes to retirement planning.

Sustainable Fulfillment

In retirement, the focus is normally on sustainability of your funds, your investments, your money flow over time. You can find every possible piece of information and advice around the slow and steady concept when it comes to retirement financial planning, but what about sustainable fulfillment? Finding long-term fulfillment with what you have built, embarked upon and initiated is about keeping the momentum in an easy, structured manner. Finding the thing that can support your goals and is a method for long-term growth is a smart way to organize your thoughts. Your exquisitely bored can morph into different versions to sustain your lifestyle, your ability to keep learning and your passions. It doesn't have to be a literal or linear path. What does need to be linear, in my experience, are the principles and passion driving your mindset.

Being Overwhelmingly Good at Everything

Are some of you good at many things? It can be overwhelming to narrow down your focus to what is the one thing you can focus on for maximum meaning.

There isn't a shortcut to landing on your thing, and it may take ideation and a few tries to see what sticks. Once you've found it, it's also important to keep evolving and tapping into new creative ideas that your target audience may be open to.

Is it Talent or is it Passion?

You can be really good at something or have exceptional talent at something but it's not always your passion. This is an interesting way to look at things because which one is more likely to drive success and value for you? Which of these can sustain us over the long-term into retirement to act as your guide? Both of these, it turns out, need to play into your long-term sustainable plan. If you focus on your passion, you may need more learning and tools for building aptitude to make money at your passion. You may need to learn a new skill that allows you to work with the things that make you passionate. Your natural learning self can acquire and develop such skills in order to build something of value.

The Fractional Future

Everything is moving in the direction of fractional employment. Even ad agencies are looking at downsizing and instead finding talent from a pool of people working fractionally across a multitude of skill sets. Your talent and passion could be a fractional role in which you provide your value to many using fractional pieces of your skill set. The exciting possibility about this approach is the opportunity to work with multiple clients and many businesses across a variety of products and services. Your value becomes about focus at a particular time, on a particular project that allows you to work across many categories. Talk about keeping the continuous learning box checked!

Variety is the spice of life, and having many talents and passions is a retirement dream. Perhaps your business is about offering a menu of abilities, and coupled with your work experience, it makes you a retired Swiss army knife of services. People are busy and distracted, and technology is giving us answers for where and what we can focus on for maximum fulfillment return. As more people work remotely, these fractional roles are becoming the common answer for all sizes of businesses. Being able to work anywhere, anytime, is a benefit that the retired demographic brings to the table that no other generation can. With a desire and drive to stay interesting and relevant, we are truly at an advantage for how we work, and the choices we make to fulfill our dreams. It sounds lofty, but in actual fact, the world has changed to securely benefit the intellectual capital we are sitting on as retirees.

Key Takeaways:

It feels like we need to keep building momentum, but it's okay to check in with our fulfillment factor to ensure we are still doing meaningful work. Sustainable fulfillment is as important as financial.

Many successes achieved by others involve a slow and steady, methodical path leading to incremental accomplishments.

The fractional movement is a benefit in that people can work from anywhere and enjoy a variety of roles, skills and experience.

Reflections:

Are you good at a variety of things? Can you reflect on how to narrow the possibilities down for an area of focus?

Does being passionate about something mean you have the talent for it?

Is it passion or talent that is likely to drive value for you?

Finding Your Exquisitely Bored: Actions

1. What things are you passionate about that would require you to further develop your talent?

2. Can you identify a technology that would benefit you to learn about?

3. Have you been able to identify the things that you spend time on that provide the highest return for your efforts?

EXQUISITELY BORED BLESSINGS

"I don't mind running with turtles." – Sondra Faye

....

"Slow down. Calm down. Don't worry. Don't hurry. Trust the process." – Alexandra Stoddard

....

"Long term consistency triumphs short term intensity." – Bruce Lee

....

"Pause and remember – Slow and steady will get you where you want to go. If you put too much pressure on yourself for results too quickly, you will quickly give up." – Jennifer Young

....

"To make the quickest progress, you don't have to take huge leaps. You just have to take baby steps– and keep on taking them. In Japan, they call this approach kaizen, which literally translates as 'continual improvement.' Using kaizen, great and lasting success is achieved through small, consistent steps. It turns out that slow and steady is the best way to overcome your resistance to change." – Marci Shimoff

....

"So stay true to your own nature. If you like to do things in a slow and steady way, don't let others make you feel as if you have to race. If you enjoy depth, don't force yourself to seek breadth. If you prefer sin-gle–tasking to multi–tasking, stick to your guns. Being relatively unmoved by rewards gives you the incalcu-lable power to go your own way." – Susan Cain

....

"Nothing contributes so much to tranquilize the mind as a steady purpose – a point on which the soul may fix its intellectual eye." – Mary Shelley

....

CHAPTER 17
PHASE 12: THE REWARD

*"Give people one thing that makes their life
easier and reward will follow."*
– Exquisitely Bored

What about getting paid for what you are good at?
How is life suddenly less expensive just because
you are retired? There is an element of finding un-
paid fulfillment, but I firmly believe you all have mad
skills that people will reward financially. I have long
believed that money is connected to personal fulfillment. And while there are variables like having your
health and healthy relationships, money is a way to
ease stress and financial insecurity. It is also a way
to find fulfillment when it comes to loved ones and
friends from a vantage point of demonstrating gener-
osity, giving reward, taking leadership, and having a
sense of pride to support a financial moment in time.

Receiving Value for Goods Delivered

Once you tap into your talent and passion and have a way forward for your business, a return to a different type of work or a continuation of your current path of employment, there is no reason you should not be receiving value for your skills. No age, gender or circumstance should dictate your inability to receive payment for what you are offering. Tapping into that knowledge base. Offering a service or product and being rewarded in return all goes toward developing a sense of pride and accomplishment. With that also comes meaning for your efforts and satisfaction in having built an alternate income stream.

Money Psychology

Your money DNA typically comes from how you were raised, regarding how you perceive money, the value you put on money and how you use your money. This likely will translate into your retirement and could have an effect on the age at which you are reading this book, but it doesn't matter because money is money and we all like to make it, have it and spend it! Whatever your prerogative with money, the important thing is to visualize being paid for the thing you are finding fulfillment in. Aligning our principles with our money intake is a great way to be able to put money back into our exquisitely bored. That can include building a better website to market our services and buying business-related products and services or marketing dollars. Your money for services rendered is how you can make your exquisitely bored manifest larger than you imagined.

If you can relate to your money based on your principles and passions, then you can know alignment. This can in turn drive your initiative forward positively. It can even have fulfillment attached to it. When your money connects to the thing fulfilling you, and I mean real meaningful fulfillment, then use that to further fuel your awareness and shift. Your definition and relationship to money with heart alignment will be different than if it is based on a materialistic premise. It instead can be a powerful facilitator for everything your business, learning and daily work represents. Money can become a fulfillment facilitator and not the source.

Confidence To Be Paid

As we age, confidence can deteriorate. We no longer have an open mind to the same things and we prefer the safety and security of the everyday. However, when you begin to realize the skills and knowledge you have, you can picture the money following. If you are clear on what you are delivering and have a clear value proposition and succinct explanation for your product or service, guess what? Nobody cares how old you are. Fixed thinking is limited, but by being re-latable and putting yourself out there instead of over-thinking, you can get on with it. Being able to think differently about money and reprogramming previ-ous conceptions will take work. But once you manage to see the world for what it is, work from anywhere, access to information and learning at your fingertips, you can reframe your mindset about what after re-tirement can mean for you.

Your Value Exchange

Exchanging your value for money can be simple. You just need to give people one thing that makes their life easier. You managed to get to the FU intersec-tion now you can bring that same hustle into view and start revisualizing what making money looks like after retirement. A lot of these references, phrases and sayings are just coined from the status quo; they don't hold any power over your life. I see so many vibrant retirees just biding time and following a pro-tocol of what they think retirement is supposed to be. These archaic notions are holding a lot of people back. Beautiful, exquisitely bored people have the magic to unleash so much potential! Stop using your age as an excuse, stop feeding the system and start focusing on your value.

The Long Game

We are living longer, and with the average age of retirement in Canada being 64, a lot of people won't be able to afford all the surprises retired life throws at them financially. But it's not even about money if you think about how many years you could actually live, and what is it that you are living for? You could spend more than 20 years engaging in meaningless activities. Activities like sports are great for our social system, but when we think of deep, meaningful fulfillment there has to be a focus on greater depth of living content. The trap of doing "dumb things" is wide open, between scroll time, letting your physical health slip, watching mainstream news, living in isolation—all of these contribute potentially to an unfulfilled passage of time.

If our socialization consists of others with the same systemic habits, there isn't much incentive or benchmark to be working towards. Feeling lost is common, and those who we choose to spend our time with will formulate our belief system in retirement and fuel wherever and whatever we are focused on. The exquisitely bored look for more: They seek joy, structure, healthy lifestyle and others who challenge their ideas and notions of what a traditional retirement looks like. The long game is about building new routines, making new connections and expecting more from yourself than maybe you ever have in your life. Plowing through self-doubt to mobilize and engage is the life force that can drive a sense of accomplishment. Find your thing and pursue it to your death, literally. This is your final pronouncement and you deserve to be seen, heard and paid!

Key Takeaways:

It's okay to collect money as a reward for your skills and as a result receive fulfillment from that exchange.

Age should not be a factor in determining what monetary reward you can receive for your skills.

The exquisitely bored seek new routines, connections and incentives. They strive for deeper living and challenge the ideas and notions around traditional retirement.

Reflections:

What things are you really good at that you can envision receiving payment for?

What skills do you think are limited by age?

What scares you the most when you think about retirement?

Finding Your Exquisitely Bored: Actions

1. Research and competitively compare how to best price your services.

2. Pick a couple of connections from your network and ask for input on your pricing structure.

3. Write down the three things that are currently giving you the highest sense of satisfaction and meaning.

EXQUISITELY BORED
BLESSINGS

"Success seems to be connected with action. Successful people keep moving. They make mistakes, but they don't quit." – Conrad Hilton

....

"Success is the sum of small efforts, repeated day in and day out." – Robert Collier

....

"Talent is nothing without persistence."
– Dean Crawford

....

"Motivation will almost always beat mere talent."
– Norman Ralph Augustine

....

"Let me tell you the secret that has led me to my goals: my strength lies solely in my tenacity."
– Louis Pasteur

....

"Start where you are. Use what you have. Do what you can." – Arthur Ashe

....

"I'm a great believer in luck, and I find the harder I work the more of it I have." – Thomas Jefferson

....

"Discipline is the bridge between goals and accomplishment." – Jim Rohn

....

"When your dreams include service to others – accomplishing something that contributes to others – it also accelerates the accomplishment of that goal. People want to be part of something that contributes and makes a difference." – Jack Canfield

....

"Self–image sets the boundaries of individual accomplishment." – Maxwell Maltz

....

"Every great work, every big accomplishment, has been brought into manifestation through holding to the vision, and often just before the big achievement, comes apparent failure and discouragement."
– Florence Scovel Shinn

....

"Well–being cannot exist just in your own head. Well–being is a combination of feeling good as well as actually having meaning, good relationships and accomplishment." – Martin Seligman

....

"It had long since come to my attention that people of accomplishment rarely sat back and let things happen to them. They went out and happened to things." – Elinor Smith

....

"The supreme accomplishment is to blur the line between work and play." – Arnold J. Toynbee

....

CHAPTER 18
PHASE 13: STAY FOCUSED STAY TRUE

"Know the distance ahead of time, stay the course and yet be willing to go further."
– Exquisitely Bored

Staying true is about the principles I talk about in previous chapters. When you stay true to yourself and what really makes you feel whole, it won't always be the popular choice. Retirement is a tough one because this demographic becomes comfortable with familiarity. Factors like technology have changed the concept of work, and the notion of retirement has to change along with that. Established routines are what most retirees will fall back on. A comfortable sense of how retirement "should be." As you further track your goals and ambitions, there are going to be people who don't align with your objectives. Your expectations are different; you will see joy and contentment differently than your peers. Protecting your time is difficult, especially if you have already retired and are returning to the workforce or starting your own business.

Prioritizing and Setting Boundaries

In order to maintain your focus, setting boundaries becomes necessary. Other retirees who have different interests will need to understand this new version of you. Boundaries are simply another way you are loving yourself. It's okay to not feel the same camaraderie with your retired peers. You may have ideas about what you can create, build, start, sell and explore among other ambitions. You can't just rely on the people around you to offer meaning and purpose. You have to put the work in to find the passions that drive you and the energy to push the benchmark for yourself.

Remembering Your Strengths

When you start doubting yourself, focus on your strengths. Revisit talent and passion in your thoughts and dwell on where you know you shine. Your strengths are unique to you and have nothing to do with being retired. Building on your current strengths is the easiest way to navigate your path to new things. Maybe you decide to continue your depth of knowledge around something you are passionate about. This is a good starting point because your confidence and comfort level will be secure. If you are starting a business, hobby or course, think big about what you want in return. I think being paid for something you can offer others is a goal that all retired people can aspire to. You are only fighting a system that dictates life to be a certain way, and you are not tied to this school of thought. The exquisitely bored are outliers: they seek more fulfillment, bigger, more in-depth lives and have the courage to at least try. Wasn't the founder of McDonald's in his 50s when he started his business? Limiting ourselves with age numbers, and what society tells us should be a time to "retire" from work related activities, means we narrow our thinking, and it's easy to slip into what I refer to as being busy "doing stupid things." Trust yourself and lean into the tension of finding change and new perspectives.

Welcome Change and Personal Growth

Once you start practicing change and personal growth and however that manifests for you, you will find your mind is more elastic than you realize. When you become aware of the newfound flexibility and the many ways you can stretch your mind, you realize it's simply practice! Your brain is always able to keep learning, and the fixed mindset that we are taught to succumb to in retirement is a very dangerous place to get stuck in. When there are so many others around you who are retired, becoming part of the stasis is easier than fighting upstream. It's natural to seek comfort and familiarity. But you can't fight that uncomfortable feeling of knowing you are meant for more.

Retirement is an extremely personal process. Variables we can't always control are often at the helm. However we find ourselves at the intersection of winding down, we must fight the tendency to simply disengage. The exquisitely bored are likely to aim higher; it's not simply about travel and social activities, but rather how can I be more? How can I be bold, fearless and even naïve about the possibilities? What we don't know won't hurt us at this stage. I think we make up the age thing and the misguided perceptions that accompany age. I'm not sure it's as real as we are supposed to think. When something becomes a societal norm, it steers us to conformity. Societal norms are restrictive and harmful to an ambitious person's way of thinking. Curtailing and suppressing are both words that come to mind when I think of the system that retirement typically entails. I don't think this has to reflect our reality, and I think we are wired for more. Maybe we just need to hear it or read it. I do know that it's difficult to take the road less travelled. Other retired peers will likely not understand your desire not to simply accept the same things they are doing.

Aspire Down Aim Up

However you aspire in age, societal constructs tend to work against our aspirations. Each generation has its zeitgeist of beliefs and ideas. What if you were to aspire to other trends, topics and ideas within different generations? The rule book has changed. It is no longer acceptable to just play it safe and still be respected and admired. Having the cool confidence of an older demographic now has a place across all platforms and social settings. The traditional notions of things like retirement and age are being replaced with opportunity and relevance and are even becoming cool! Intergenerational considerations like fashion, art, entertainment and brands are seeing opportunities with cross marketing and communications to stand out from the crowd and to present a juxtaposition of unique and special value propositions that include an older generation. With people working longer, multi-generations are inhabiting the work force and combining to build a greater understanding and tolerance across all ages.

But the more we feed into the systemic expectations based on age, the further we stunt and enforce archaic and outdated ideas and developments. When technology makes it so seamless to work anywhere, anytime, it's easy to offer a product or service behind a keyboard, and does anyone even need to know about how age factors into the average transaction? The people who will survive the modernization of this way of thinking and process any and all possibilities will benefit from increased working years, additional income and a healthy mind and spirit. When you think of the learning, years of experience and playbook of tried-and-true methods of both failure and success that we possess as retirees, there is a wealth of information and input on the table for future generations. The principles of business remain the same. However we help a new generation interpret those can be our legacy. I don't think we have enough focus on mentoring and passing our intel on to the future. Does this ideal not mitigate the fears a little for those nearing retirement or already there? Mentoring and connecting are key to staying relevant and interesting. Tapping into the younger mindset allows us to aspire down in an energetic and open-minded manner. At the same time, we aim higher not to simply be content with retirement as we know it traditionally. The exquisitely bored will not go willingly; we will aspire beyond the traditional definitions and test the narrative that has so long been in place. We are the thinkers, the doers and the builders. Let's align principles with passion. Let's find our people and start connecting for a new era of living, speaking and being. The exquisitely bored are everywhere; they are among us and actively reinventing the world as we know it.

Key Takeaways:

Setting boundaries allows you to track your goals and ambitions. Boundaries provide you with the space and time to focus on the things you are holding yourself accountable for.

Focus on your strengths. Remember, you are only as limited as the system would like you to think you are.

Societal constructs work against our aspirations. We can reinvent the world as we know it and aspire beyond the traditional narratives.

Reflections:

What examples can you think of in which society places limitations based on age?

Have you noticed that where you find fulfillment is different from your peers?

Are there certain types of people that require more boundaries than others? What do you think is missing for them in retirement?

Finding Your Exquisitely Bored: Actions

1. Can you think of a couple of examples where you notice you have strengthened your skill set from simply practicing it more?

2. Are there any specific new perspectives that you have developed?

3. Can you note areas of expertise that you could offer mentoring in? Find someone in your network who could benefit from your experience and input.

EXQUISITELY BORED BLESSINGS

"What you stay focused on will grow."
– Roy T. Bennett

....

"Where your attention goes, your time goes"
– Idowu Koyenikan

....

"Instead of focusing on how much you can accomplish, focus on how much you can absolutely love what you're doing." – Leo Babauta

....

"When you fully focus your mind, you make others attracted to you." – Toba Beta

....

"Concentrate all your thoughts upon the work in hand. The sun's rays do not burn until brought to a focus." – Alexander Graham Bell

....

"The ability to concentrate and to use time well is everything." – Lee Iacocca

....

"The more focused you are, the more successful you will be." – Tony Robbins

"The greatest weapon against stress is our ability to choose one thought over another." – William James

"Productivity is never an accident. It is always the result of a commitment to excellence, intelligent planning, and focused effort." – Paul J. Meyer

"Juggling, multitasking, and other forms of 'attention shifting' are highly inefficient. Simply, the brain works much faster and more accurately when attention is focused, for a stretch of time, on one thing at a time." – Harvard Business Review

"Complexity means distracted effort. Simplicity means focused effort." – Edward De Bono

"Simplicity of approach is always best."
– Charlie Chaplin

CHAPTER 19
RISE: RETIRE INSIGHT SEEK EARN

"Retire, gain insight, seek and earn.
It's permission to write a new history."
- Exquisitely Bored

Many of you are likely familiar with the FIRE movement: Financial Independence Retire Early. Just as this movement saw devotees with a belief system and philosophy around employing money methods to retire sooner than later, I subscribe to a term that I have coined called, RISE: Retire Insight Seek and Earn. RISE embodies the premise of "Exquisitely Bored: Finding Fulfillment in Retirement" as a story and mindset. Seeing retirement more as a continuous process throughout our lives instead of one final stage means it can become more of an individual choice, experience and way of achieving multiple goals. When we define something in a new way, we give people permission to change and adjust. Change their thinking, change their behaviour and change their actions.

We are taught about permissions at an early age. Society has created invisible social structures that guide and provide permission for its members to align with a certain thinking, process and predictability factors when it comes to how we act and what we do at a certain age. But not everyone's everyday experiences are the same based on age. Interests and abilities are diverse, circumstances vary and differences exist across the entire human spectrum, not just within a particular segment. When you think of the decade in which many of our older generation would have grown up, they have seen and been involved in more movements, upheaval and resistance to authority than many other generations ever will. They fought the establishment for change, shifted society's thinking and brought about counterculture. They continue today to challenge timelines, expectations and social currency.

Younger generations will not be able to meet the established retirement definitions that are in place. Many variables are driving this, stemming from housing costs, student debt, starting families later in life, access to investing earlier and a host of other generational challenges. It likely will deteriorate from there for future generations.

Retiring Retirement

The opportunity to start talking about retirement differently and to adopt a way of thinking that has society preparing earlier, socially and emotionally, is increasingly catching on. Expanding the definition of "preparing" to beyond the financial is imperative so that those pre- and in retirement have more options for continued learning and can still enjoy meaningful employment. It might be time to retire the traditional word retirement as we know it. Future workers will have different needs, and ideally if an individual decides to keep working, we will have fostered a culture of support for that individual and others who are so inclined. I'm not suggesting we remove the option to retire—I'm simply promoting the concept of continued work lifestyle.

Mental Health

The benefits of working longer have many long reaching advantages that can keep our population engaged in healthy ways, from cognitive awareness and stimulation to a sense of purpose, structure and routine. In previous chapters I speak to a sense of self-worth, self-value and self-hope, all of which contribute to overall quality of life and an engaged society.

Living Longer and Living Younger

When you look at the average retirement age, you realize that we have more healthy years in front of us compared to previous generations. Education and dialogue around physical health, fitness and diet have us living longer and challenging age-related physical stereotypes. As a result, we are essentially living younger as we age down in attitude and aspirations.

Remote Work Options

The new work world now offers increased capacity to work longer when you can work from your desired location in a variety of roles. Re-evaluating how people work has allowed older workers to remain engaged with physicality removed from roles that can be done remotely. This has provided an aging population with increased flexibility and work-life balance as the traditional office commute has disappeared entirely in some cases.

Financial Benefit

Future generations that may not have the means for financial independence at the age the system has established will be able to extend their share of wallet by working longer. Working longer presents options for an older generation to financially aid children and extended family in a time when housing and other expenses have driven the cost of living up and certain lifestyle choices are now out of reach for new workers. Having access to additional sources of financial means for longer ensures that all can benefit from the safety net of working family members.

Positive Aging Attitudes

More work needs to be done on the topic of ageism, particularly when it comes to seeing the older population as a resource. When we think of the vast amount of volunteering done by older members of society as well as caregiving, we can see the need to develop positive beliefs and dialogue when it comes to age-related conversations. We still have a lot to combat when it comes to how we perceive aging on a personal level. One of the things I talk about earlier in the book is the segregation factor. We would have improved intergenerational relationships if we increased our socialization across the generation divide. The interaction on both sides is imperative for the proper interpretation of what ageing means in a positive light. It's such an individual process and age does not represent one consistent definition.

RISE means instead of planning for the traditional retirement, we choose instead to achieve alignment with values, passion and talent. In that, we can discover our heart-centred earning power. It means we give permission to an already retired generation to continue working, move in and out of the retirement phase if they so desire and discover untapped potential and interests. Can we give permission to work without thinking someone needs the money? Can we rethink our impressions of societal frameworks to see working beyond being a financial gap filler? The word "fulfillment" itself has two meanings as per Oxford Languages: a feeling of happiness and satisfaction but also the "completion of something like the fulfillment of a promise. The meeting of a requirement or condition." Meeting this requirement of fulfillment in our next phase means we realize all the possibilities with intention.

Is Perception Reality?

Does our perception have a view that some job roles are too important to retire from? Do we have the impression that roles like doctors, lawyers and leaders of large businesses can keep working because those are important places for people to be regardless of age? Do we treat professions like these as belonging more to an older, more practiced, more knowing group? I have observed that there seems to be more permission and less rigidity when it comes to an older segment continuing on in these careers. In fact, let's cast our attention to roles typically held by politicians. Age acts as a prerequisite for having the experience, networks and leadership markers in this particular profession. The perceived value that age brings to these particular examples has shaped society's acceptance and versatility around age being a negative factor. How do we start to give the same permission to the worker doing what we perceive to be less of a job? Perception pertaining to what a "lesser job" is doesn't mean that person is any less fulfilled than the person earning more and perceived to be in a more important role.

The Evolutionary Path Of Fulfillment

Primally, fulfillment was tied to staying alive. It correlated to contributing as a member of your tribe and relating to your role within that tribe. It meant being useful, providing for others and survival. Fulfillment is still deeply tied to our sense of well-being, achievement and productivity. Couple this with over 120 years of what our current frame of reference for retirement is, and we can start to understand we have lost sight of where fulfillment comes from. Perhaps this is why we must go through the phases I've outlined in previous chapters, to fully understand, comprehend and embrace our reality of what retirement means for us on a deeply personal level.

I think it is here in the phase of A Quiet Mind and A Still State where we start to wrestle with the inconsistencies and the mixed messaging that starts to formulate. Only through The Awakening and Acceptance phases can we discover and own the deeply provoking thoughts and ideas that start emerging. Sitting in the raw authenticity of The Shift phase causes us to move towards personal growth and action. Is it the old adage that sitting with darkness ironically provides clarity? That deep introspection can provide answers that lead to action. For our entire work lives we have likely rejected a sense of ourselves as a whole. With work-life balance, financial stressors and career conformity, we have likely lost sight of some of our own creativity, well-being and individuality. The phases allow oneself to fully appreciate and trust the process. Remember there is an entire world outside of our limited thinking and the dogma around tradiational retirement.

Choices Not Constructs

Seeing the next life phase as a choice rather than a construct gives you agency and permission to lead your set of outcomes. Don't be tied to a deadline tied to an age. Age has nothing to do with everything I've talked about in this book! Plan for a continued span of time that encompasses: career, career continuation, continuous learning and your own version of what your *what's next* looks like. Fulfillment is far reaching— it's tied to our life purpose and our core values, and work or work-like activity meets these needs so that we may connect with the world more profoundly. I see it now, I see it in the hardware store aisles, I see it in the grocery stores and I see it at law firms behind desks, and I saw it in the eyes of my previous 80-year-old dermatologist. The river of fulfillment runs deep and knows no age, the breadth of a meaningful life holds the size of the world and a sense of purpose is as big as a universe of heartfelt living. The exquisitely bored are amongst us, living extraordinary lives, writing their own stories, selling, creating, contributing and recognizing that age and purpose are completely separate. This is the RISE process, the permission you needed to find your own exquisitely bored. Stay relevant, stay interesting and stay engaged. Find your principles, your passions and your people; therein lies the answer for your own beautiful exquisitely bored blessings!

ABOUT THE AUTHOR

From the fields of a rural Ontario farm to Bogotá, Colombia as a Rotary Exchange Student to the largest board rooms globally, Joanne has seen the world through diverse and curious eyes. She has over 25 years of marketing and PR experience in global roles with some of the world's largest brands. Her experience leading high performing teams spans both private and public sectors.

She is the founder of Exquisitely Bored, through which she creates engaging and innovative content strategies for home and lifestyle brands. Joanne believes that a well curated home, full of personal expression, is fundamental to living the good life. Her philosophy embodies that your home is an evolving, magical place and that you can find style in everything around you. She believes that exquisitely bored is a mindset and a lifestyle. It is a state of experiencing the world by surrounding yourself with beautiful things and moments that create impact and leave a stylish impression.

Joanne divides her time between Stoney Lake, Ontario and Naples, Florida. Both are beautiful, inspiring environments that spark joy, creativity and ideas for Joanne's content and lifestyle. She enjoys nothing more than creating and building her client's brands and hopes to inspire others to find their version of exquisitely bored. As her grandfather would have said, "What a production!"

Website: exquisitelybored.com

Instagram: @exquisitely.bored

Email: joanne@exquisitelybored.com

LinkedIn: /in/joanne2/

Facebook: facebook.com/joanne.clark.370177

X: @ExquisiteBored

Bluesky: @exquisitelybored

ACKNOWLEDGEMENTS

I'd like to acknowledge my husband, Rich, who has worn the hat of editor and proofreader through this process. The pen behind your ear has become your signature look! I appreciate all of your help, insight and the many discussions we have engaged in to get this project across the finish line. Our deep connection built on similar beliefs, thoughts and pursuits is what keeps us curious about the world and each other.

Thank you, Samantha and Simar from Lucky Book Publishing, for your genius and bringing me into the most wonderful author community! You truly are dream makers! I'd also like to acknowledge Ellie who has been with me throughout this process, always consistent and always coaching!

Thank you to my clients who believe in exquisitely bored and where we can go from here! Tim and Chris, the way our paths crossed is the perfect example of how the law of attraction works. You are not just a chapter in my book!

To Vivian and our many world travels! Thank you for re-emerging as a powerful force throughout this experience. I want to be just like you!

thank you

Thank you for reading my book!

Dear Reader,

Thank you for taking the time to read my book! I appreciate your interest and curiosity to learn more about the phases, the process and the winding road that leads to finding your "what's next" in retirement! I believe in your ideas and your ability to find great fulfillment in whatever your exquisitely bored may be.

I know that having this conversation and dialogue about how to challenge traditional thinking around retirement will enlighten and encourage many of all ages. I want to ask a small favour!

Would you consider leaving a positive Amazon review? It would help to bring further discovery for this topic. Others may be able to benefit earlier on in their career path or even not feel so alone if they are currently seeking support for their next term. Your review may provide permission for someone entering retirement to find a new version of what they enjoy doing and they may be able to receive value for their skills! What an empowering way to connect with others and to be honest with oneself about finding your own exquisitely bored!

Thank you,
Joanne

MY GIFT TO YOU

I am so glad you're here!

As my gift to you, get FREE access to the audiobook of Exquisitely Bored: Finding Fulfillment in Retirement by scanning the QR Code below or visiting

www.exquisitelybored.com/the-book